I0531887

Wisdom Keeper

My Extraordinary Journey to Unlock the Sacred Within

Chloe Kemp

Awaken Your Divine Path Press

Awaken Your Divine Path Press
Arden, North Carolina

http://www.ChloeKempWisdomKeeper.com

Copyright @ 2022 by Chloe Kemp. All rights reserved.
Cover Art by Wendy Andrew - https://www.paintingdreams.co.uk

Poem by Caleb Beissert –

https://beissertpoetry.wordpress.com

Author Photo by Cat Ford-Coates - https://www.catfordcoates.com

Excerpts from "101 Ways to Heal the Earth" used with permission by Dr. Robert Gilman, President, Context Institute.

All rights reserved, including the right to reproduce this book or portions thereof in any form whatsoever without the prior written permission of Awaken Your Divine Path Press, except where permitted by law.

This memoir is a compilation of the author's recollections of personal experiences. The information is true and complete to the best of the author's knowledge. Some names and identifying details have been changed to protect the identity of certain people. Any advice or recommendations are made without guarantee on the part of the author or publisher. The author and publisher disclaim any liability in connection with the use of the information in this book. The information presented is the author's opinion and does not constitute medical or health advice and is not intended to diagnose, treat, cure or prevent any condition or disease. The ideas and suggestions in this book are not meant to be a substitute for seeking professional guidance. Please consult your physician.

Awaken Your Divine Path Press - print edition May 2022

Library of Congress Cataloging-in-Publication Data
Wisdom Keeper: My Extraordinary Journey to Unlock the Sacred Within/Chloe Kemp

Library of Congress Control Number: 2022904915

ISBN (Print): 979-8-9858269-0-6
ISBN (Ebook): 979-8-9858269-1-3

Advance Praise

"Chloe's heartfelt journey is the real deal here to inspire us all. Showing us the power of spiritual healing and the connection between the challenges we are faced with and how those are here to awaken us to our greatness. She takes the reader on a journey of darkness to light, struggle to freedom, fear to love. Thank you, Chloe, for this incredible ride. A must-read for all who want true transformation."

—Dr. Shannon South, Award-Winning Therapist, Best-Selling Author, and Founder of the Ignite Your Life and business programs

"Every experience written by Chloe in her spiritual memoir has a healing purpose. She shares processes for healing in the physical, emotional and spiritual realms, showing us our ability to use all levels of energy to achieve deep and lasting healing. Chloe reveals to us the importance of connection—with the spiritual world, physical world, and our past lives to the present. She reminds us we are essential in the Universe; when we heal, our loved ones, people around us, and the Earth also heal. Chloe shows why it is important to be connected to both the elements of earth and the elements of the cosmic world. She shares how she uses physical, emotional, and spiritual healing energy to free herself from struggle and trauma. Chloe inspires us to do the same thing. Well done. I appreciate it very much. This book is truly for everyone."

—Eduardo Morales, Shamanic Curandero, Tepoztlán, Morelos, Mexico

"WISDOM KEEPER is filled with wonderful personal experiences on the power of healing, visualizations, dreams, and listening to our inner voices. Chloe Kemp describes encounters with others on a multitude of levels, including sacred beings, shamans, and other deep-souled humans. This book inspires the reader to go deep within themselves and invite their own personal self-healer to emerge. Chloe helps us to understand that anything is possible."

—**River Guerguerian, Sound Immersion Healer, Musician, Composer, and Educator**

"Having met and worked with Chloe personally, I know she is a genuine woman with a mission and clear determination to fulfill her purpose in this life. She has followed the call from Spirit to not only share stories from her life and wisdom she has gained, but to weave energies and express a frequency of consciousness that has a way of bringing her reader to a deeper state of awareness and potency upon their own unique journey. Chloe's book shines a light on our ability to reconnect with the origin of what makes us each a special part of the Divine plan, and she does it in a very humble and approachable way."

—**Michael Brasunas, Holistic Energy Healer**

"This was so good! Very entertaining, awakening, and engaging, as well as informative and practical. You have a nice conversational tone that is also motivating and inspiring. It feels like you are sharing information with a good friend. The pacing was very good; there were no slow parts. You have a way of making all of the information relevant and interesting, as if you are speaking directly to the reader instead of to a vague, general audience. A lot of people may be new to your ideas, and you do an excellent job of communicating those ideas and relating them to actual occurrences in your life. You present a strong case, through illustrating the benefits to your own life, of why all of this should be of concern to readers, and how it can help them in their own lives. This is a great book on how to live a fuller, happier, more peaceful life that will benefit yourself and others in the world." **—Susan, USA**

"The narrative is immensely raw and deeply personal. The lucidity of the language and the effortless flow quietly got under my skin. It was thought-provoking, hopeful, and came with a tinge of suspense at the same time. I felt invested, and it engaged all of my emotions completely. The awe was real!"

—Abantika, India

"Your strength of clarity and ease leapt from every page. There were no dips or chapters that didn't meet the high standards that you set. It always appeared that the reader's experience was at the forefront of your mind, even in the dialogue, which was always clear and easy to flow. Every word uttered had a purpose. Your writing voice is smooth, complementing your content well. It pulls the reader into the events and the essence of your message, immersing them into your world. Using your own experiences to affirm your point helped to build a personal relationship with your reader. All of your characters had a purpose and drove the narrative forward. The flow of time and the sense of a journey made me keen to find out what you would learn and experience next."

—Matt, UK

"As many people said, you have a gift for spiritual healing. You also have a gift for telling a story. I was thoroughly engaged and truly believed in this story. You have a wonderful conversational tone. I feel you are talking directly to the reader, which invites them in even more to the story you are telling. The tone of the book is very hopeful and sincere, with encouraging messages of being your authentic self. You have created a compelling, interesting, and important story." **—Jessica, USA**

"Your inspiring memoir is engaging and thought-provoking throughout. It brings together the highest spiritual insights and practical frameworks that everyone can understand and apply. I'm sure it will be well received." **—Louise, Australia**

"The pacing and flow of the story are perfect! I could imagine every scene in my mind. The writing style is amazing. Everything made sense. Your life experiences are so unique. I felt I was in a magical world where miracles can happen. Your story is inspirational and motivational." **—Taibaya, Pakistan**

"This book is a fascinating read!" **—Caleb, USA**

"This intriguing book is beautifully written. It has truly been eye-opening. I've been questioning how many of my own issues would make sense or be closer to being solved if I found a healer like Chloe or the ones she mentions in her books."

—Megahlee, India

"You retell events, dreams, and moments in your life in a very engaging way that is not only enjoyable, but also thought-provoking." **—Josh, USA**

"As everyone has their ups and downs, WISDOM KEEPER will help to turn illness into health and weakness into strength. Chloe, a beautiful soul, shares her life experiences and challenges in a simple conversational style. She teaches that an open mind and the power of thought can heal any situation."

—Aneela, Pakistan

"Your story is quite remarkable." **—Michael, USA**

Dedication

I dedicate this book to everyone I have encountered on my spiritual journeys. Special thanks to my son, Cameron, who has continued to encourage and support me to grow and heal.

Contents

———————— ⌘⌘⌘ ————————

A Light Shines

By Caleb Beissert

It doesn't help to worry
you must think
you got this
you can do this

when you think
I'd like a drink of water
your hand picks up the glass
raises it to your lips

you're riding on an infinite wave
put your finger in the water
see how it creates
more tiny waves

you can see the reflection
of stars but if you try
to touch them they disappear

we can be the waves
guiding each other
we can be the storm
we turn away from

turn to the sunny beaches
at the edge of time
turn to the orchards
where we rested in summer

turn your thoughts
to what heals you
even in the darkness

Introduction

One day when I was playing with my two-year-old son, he turned toward me and asked, "What took you so long?"

I responded, "Took me so long to do what?"

With no hesitation, he answered, "I had to wait a very long time for you to be ready for me to come here and be born."

He looked at me like his words were as routine as asking me what we would have for dinner.

I understood what he meant but still found it "mind-boggling" that my two-year-old son was talking to me about past lives. His question did not alarm or scare me; the concept of past lives was not new to me. I had been having past life regressions since my twenties. When you use a past life regression therapist, they take you to a relaxed hypnotic state to explore your past.

I remembered reading that it is not uncommon for some children to remember previous lives.

I asked him, "What else do you remember?"

His response made me a firm believer in past lives as he began describing a planet where he had lived. He gave the exact details of a place I had seen during a past life regression about five years earlier. We both remembered an advanced planet with sophisticated technology and telepathic communication.

Before this conversation, I still had some uncertainty about reincarnation. When my son, who was too young to know about the concept, started remembering other lives and could talk about it so coherently, all my doubts vanished.

It's difficult to wrap one's head around the concept of past lives. Once you are open to the possibility, patterns and connections emerge. You might meet someone new and have a strong sense of familiarity like you already know them. Or you visit a new place and have memories of being there, even though you have never visited it this lifetime. Dreams can also be a gateway to remembering other lives.

A big lesson I learned over the years is not to assume what you are remembering or "seeing" is just your imagination or random coincidence. I understand it may be challenging to remain open. In the early days of having visions and past life memories, I would preface it with, "This is crazy. Maybe I am just making it up." Gradually, I trusted myself more.

During this time, Spirit also gifted me with a way to confirm I am in the presence of the Divine. In those moments, little Divine tears well up in my eyes. The first few times it happened, I discounted it as a coincidence. Later, I began trusting this process; I love having the ability to have a "truth detector" for my spiritual work.

The first time I recalled a past life on my own was back in the early '80s, when I kept having confusing thoughts about a new friend. Every time we were together, I had visions of a life in Paris. At first, my memories seemed random. But the Paris visions and memories persisted. I never mentioned it to her since I didn't fully understand the past life connection.

Not sure what to believe, I remembered being obsessed with the cancan as a child. In the fifth grade, I choreographed and designed cancan costumes for my school talent show. I also performed the cancan in two musicals. As an adult, I once again choreographed and designed costumes and talked my friends into performing the cancan on New Year's Eve at the legendary Austin music venue, the Armadillo World Headquarters. Considering my early obsession with the cancan, and these feelings about Paris with my friend, I took a leap of faith that my memories of Paris were not just my imagination.

Thirty years later, I met a shaman while living in Ecuador. He had an instantaneous familiarity. We both began remembering multiple past lives we had together. Even more surprising, he told me he has had a recurring dream since childhood of living in Paris. He was a server, and there was always the same woman in the dream. Divine tears flowed down my cheeks as he spoke about his life in Paris. I realized I was that woman, and he must be part of the reason Paris held such significance for me. At that moment, I had a clear vision flash of being a dancer at the Moulin Rouge. Two years later, I went to Paris and received much more clarity, healing, and closure about my past life there.

How can revisiting a past life help you in this life?

The impact of events in a past life can often show up in another life. I do intuitive shamanic energy healing work, including clearing dark energy and blockages and healing emotional, mental, physical, and spiritual issues. Working with my Spirit Guides, I enter a trance state, enabling me to visit other dimensions to help with my energy healing sessions. Everyone has access to Spirit Guides or ancestors from other dimensions that show up to help you. My Spirit Guides give me direction on what to do and what parts of the body to work on during a session.

In 2010, I saw a client's past life during her energy session with me. Although I have remembered many of my past lives, I had never recalled the past lives of other people in such detail.

First, my Spirit Guides instructed me to place my left hand on her belly. Whenever I tried to place that hand somewhere else, my guides insisted I not move it. Then they instructed me to get my Native American feather headpiece from another room.

Since I do my healing work in a trance, I hesitated, as I didn't want to lose my trance state or leave her on the table. My guides kept insisting, so I quickly retrieved it. When I returned to the room, I had an immediate vision of her as a goddess in Egypt. In the vision, she was wearing an elaborate feather headdress.

As I placed my feather headpiece on her forehead, it transported me to a temple in ancient Egypt. I saw my client lying on a table in the temple; a man entered and began stabbing her in the belly. Having a difficult time killing her, he had to stab her almost twenty times before she died. Her emotions ran the gamut of fear, followed by confusion, anger, and sadness.

This was a man she knew and trusted. His betrayal overwhelmed her. I experienced her emotions during the stabbing back in Egypt so strongly that tears streamed down my face as I silently sobbed. It was like standing in as her surrogate to re-experience her death.

It amazed me how quickly the session changed once I placed the feather headdress on my client's forehead. Even though I resisted my Spirit Guides' request to go into the other room to get the headdress, it turned out to be a significant piece of information that allowed me to see my client's past life in Egypt. As a goddess, she wore an elaborate feather headpiece. As soon as I laid my feather on her forehead, her life in ancient Egypt appeared to me, as clear as watching a movie.

Honoring what Spirit guides you to do, even if logically it makes little sense, is important when dealing with the spiritual world and alternative healing. It is a way to surrender your ego and trust the Divine, which clears the way and creates space for miracles.

Afterward, I asked her if she noticed anything during the session.

"Yes, you had your hand on my belly the whole time. Usually, I don't let anyone touch my belly, not even my husband."

"That is not surprising. I saw in an ancient Egyptian lifetime that someone you knew murdered you. It took multiple stab wounds to your belly to kill you."

She responded, "Wow! Your ability to tap into my past life and clear the stabbing wound literally feels like you have removed a knife from my stomach! I have just had an amazing, empowering energy transformation. Thank you for providing a relaxing and safe environment for my energy soul healing. I am amazed that you could channel such powerful energy. I can now understand and move past my karmic struggle in that lifetime."

Chapter 1

First Major Healing Miracle

———— ༄ ༄ ༄ ————

In my late twenties, I became pregnant and had an abortion. I am pro-choice but had hoped I would never have to make that decision. Turns out, it can be much harder in actual life. My Argentinian husband was not willing to step up. In disbelief, I waited until the last moment to end my pregnancy. We already had marital problems; this was the final straw for me.

Even though he pushed me to abort, he did nothing to help me deal with this decision. Too embarrassed to ask a friend to go with me, I took a taxi. In the recovery room, I cried nonstop. I regretted my decision, but it was too late.

I had nightmares related to the abortion. One recurring dream showed me putting a baby in the garbage disposal and turning on the switch. I had frequent dreams about baby-sitting, with many disasters happening, showing me incapable of taking care of a baby.

A few years later, I developed endometriosis, a medical condition where the uterus lining grows in other body parts, causing pain and heavy bleeding. I would have exploratory surgery, they would clean everything up, and over time, I would have problems again.

After three surgeries, I found another doctor, a renowned surgeon and fertility expert. Although I was not trying to get pregnant, I wanted a doctor who had plenty of experience with endometriosis. As they were preparing me for my fourth laparoscopy, the surgeon transported me to the X-ray area to do a vaginal ultrasound. After returning to my hospital room, they gave me medicine to make me sleepy. Before they rolled me into the operating room, the surgeon stopped us in the hall.

"I am sorry to have to do this, but I noticed a significant tumor during the ultrasound. I need you to give me written permission so I can remove it."

Although drowsy from the medicine, I paused for a moment before signing the paper and said to myself, "I am done."

When they moved me from recovery to my hospital room, the surgeon came in to talk with me. What he said shocked me.

"I would like for you to tell me what happened. When I opened you up, the tumor had disappeared. The only explanation is a miracle."

He continued. "I also expected to see scar tissue from your three previous surgeries. There was none, which is also miraculous."

Still groggy from the surgery, I comprehended how significant it was for the doctor to explain this experience as a miracle. It took a while for me to understand the power and healing impact of saying "I am done" right before the surgery. At first, I thought it referred to being done with having surgeries.

Besides the endometriosis, I developed cervical stenosis, a condition where the opening to your cervix is much more narrow than is normal. I had to go through a painful procedure to open it up. Later, the doctor diagnosed pelvic inflammatory disease and uterine polyps.

My spiritual practice has taught me to wait and sit with things, allowing the answers to flow to me. At some point, everything came together. I realized the dreams and the medical problems were all related to the abortion. I was having a hard time forgiving myself.

What surprised me when I looked at the list of medical problems, I realized that all of them can cause sterility in women. I had been subconsciously doing everything in my power to never get pregnant again. I felt like I didn't deserve a baby because of the abortion.

My "I am done" moment before the fourth surgery was about me being done with punishing myself. There was no way to change it; nothing would bring that baby back. So, I said a prayer and sent love to my sweet unborn baby's soul. Two years later, I gave birth to my son.

Chapter 2

Exploring the Dream World

―――――― ⟍ᏐᏐᏽ ――――――

Dreams can be a powerful gateway to spiritual wisdom, information, Spirit Guide messages, and healing. I have experienced vivid dreams since childhood. Some seemed like premonitions that foretold the future, but I convinced myself they were just a coincidence. I could not imagine my prophetic dreams and visions were real at that point in my life.

In my twenties, I took a course on dreams, hoping to better understand an ongoing nightmare that began when I was three and continued into my adult life. It was a terrifying dream. A big boogeyman monster would crawl up between the walls and floor of my bedroom. Petrified, I would scream for help, but no one ever came to help me. So, I would start running to get away. I would wake myself up screaming, with my legs moving as fast as they could to escape.

The professor taught us how to program our dreams. Each week he had me change something in the dream. He wanted to help me empower myself in the dream. First, he suggested I ask for help from the people in the other room. When I tried that, no one came to help. So, his next suggestion was to put a gun in the dream.

"I'm sorry, I am uncomfortable with putting a gun in the dream."

He explained, "It isn't necessary to use the gun. I just want it there so you will feel safe."

"But that's the point. I am extremely anti-guns. It will not make me feel safe to put a gun in the dream."

He responded, "Okay. What about putting a dog in the dream to protect you?"

"Thanks. That sounds perfect."

"Remember, the dog is there to protect you. Since it is guarding you, there will be no need for you to run or scream. You can tell the 'boogeyman' that if he doesn't leave, the dog is going to bite him."

Wow! In hindsight, what a simple solution. The reoccurring nightmare I had been having for over twenty-four years disappeared.

Lucid dreaming

This experience of learning how to better understand and program my dreams helped me become a lucid dreamer. If you are a lucid dreamer, you experience the dream on multiple levels. At some point, you are aware you are dreaming and become an observer of the dream. You also may be in the dream. Part of you can also step back and analyze everything while dreaming. When my lucid dream is prophetic, my Spirit Guides tell me to pay attention because it is an important vision dream.

After a lucid dream when I was around twenty-four weeks pregnant, I accepted that my prophetic vision dreams were real. In this brief dream, I saw myself in the delivery room. Initially happy and excited, I noticed I wasn't doing any special childbirth breathing. Since my plans included a natural birth, that seemed strange. In the delivery room, I saw a calendar on the wall with the date September 16, 1986. I realized I wasn't doing Lamaze breathing because my baby's due date was November 27, and the birthing classes had not begun.

I woke up the next morning with slight cramping. Normally I would not have been concerned—it did not seem significant. However, because my dream showed me having my baby early, I called the doctor's office. It surprised me when they told me to come in immediately.

With my due date months away, my uterus had started thinning, and my baby had dropped into the birth canal. The doctor sent me home with instructions to stay in bed and call her the next day. Still experiencing a little cramping, when I called, the doctor told me to come back in and be prepared to go to the hospital. The exam showed I was in active labor.

I spent a week in the hospital hooked up to all kinds of machines and medicines. Nothing was working to stop the labor. At one point, they moved me to a delivery room because they thought the birth would be imminent. There was one more very experimental drug they had not tried. On September 16, the same date I saw on the calendar in my dream, that last drug stopped the labor. I spent the rest of my pregnancy on bed rest.

If it were not for the lucid dream about being in premature labor, it is likely my son would have been born at twenty-four weeks. My willingness to pay attention to the dream saved my son's life.

Since that lucid dream thirty-four years ago, there have been a plethora of prophetic vision dreams. I always honor my Spirit Guides when they tell me to pay attention to particular dreams.

Chapter 3

Devastating Diagnosis of an Incurable Illness

—⁓❧⁓—

In 2003, I noticed my feet and lower legs seemed numb much of the time. I assumed it was a circulation problem, so I saw a cardiologist. After his exam and tests, he said everything looked fine but suggested I see a neurologist.

The neurologist did some tests in his office and then sent me for an MRI. He never mentioned what all these tests might reveal. After the technician finished looking at the MRI, he asked a question that shocked me.

"How long has your doctor been thinking you have multiple sclerosis?"

I responded, "What?! No one has ever mentioned MS to me."

The tech replied, "Oh no. I am so sorry; I thought you knew."

When I discussed the results with my neurologist, he suggested doing more tests. It is difficult to be certain of a multiple sclerosis diagnosis, so he wanted to be as thorough as possible. He performed more tests in his office and then a spinal fluid tap at the hospital. Based on all the tests, the MRI, and the spinal fluid tap, and ruling out all other possibilities, I received an official MS diagnosis in the spring of 2004.

I did not panic until he told me that the thing he most dreaded telling his patients was that they had multiple sclerosis. Considering how many types of serious illnesses neurologists handle, I could no longer pretend this wasn't a big deal.

He stressed multiple sclerosis is a very serious and progressive illness and insisted I go on one of the MS medications. Within months of being on the medication, I ended up in the hospital because they thought I might be having a heart attack. The side effects of all the extra medication I used to counter the side effects of the MS drug had also caused all my liver enzymes to elevate. When I got out of the hospital, I told my doctor to take me off all the medications.

"It is bad enough that I have to deal with multiple sclerosis. I am not willing to have other organs damaged because of all the side effects of the MS meds. I will find a different way to deal with it."

Multiple sclerosis uprooted my entire life. Besides debilitating fatigue, speech and physical coordination problems, partial numbness in my extremities, blurred vision, and severe pain, I had significant cognitive issues. Before MS, people admired my mental abilities, saying my mind operated like a computer. Now I had difficulties doing even the most basic things.

After my diagnosis, a nurse came to teach me how to give myself daily shots. First, he showed me how to do it a few times. Then I watched a video. Afterwards, he showed me once again how to prepare and inject the shot. Next, he asked me to do it myself. My mind went blank. I remembered nothing. Tears rolled down my cheeks—this was the first time I realized how drastically my cognitive abilities had declined.

When someone gave me change for a dollar, and I couldn't count the money, I felt devastated. Another time, I forgot how to write a check after the cashier rang up a cart full of food at the grocery store. She had to write it for me and show me where to sign my name.

I quit working because I lacked the physical stamina and mental abilities to continue. The last few weeks before I took medical leave, it was necessary to take multiple naps to get through the day. I would get up and shower and then rest before I had enough energy to get dressed and eat. I would still need one more nap before I drove to work. During lunch and after work, I would have to go to my car for more naps.

At that point I didn't even possess the energy to go to the grocery store. Only a few blocks from my house, I was too exhausted by the time I drove there to get out of my car to shop.

My doctor gave me some cognitive tests. The results showed that when I did something that required a great deal of cognitive focus and accuracy, I only had about a thirty-minute window. If I tried pushing myself beyond my capabilities, the only result would be utter exhaustion. I made the tough decision to quit driving.

By the fall of 2004, I had become too weak to take care of myself. It was exhausting to do the most basic things, like taking a shower or brushing my teeth. At fifty-two, I was bedridden. My mother and sister were already talking about putting me in a nursing home if I didn't get better. A personal turning point for me, I vowed somehow I would get better.

I followed a diet created by Dr. Roy Swank, a neurologist specializing in multiple sclerosis. Swank created this diet before there were medications for MS. It is a very healthy way of eating for anyone. Basically, it is an anti-inflammatory diet—low fat, low sugar, and no gluten, legumes, eggs, dairy, or soy.

Yoga and gentle exercise also helped. Slowly building my strength back, thankfully, I was no longer bedridden. Although daily MS problems still plagued me, I found an alternative way to live. I would often be so sick I would be in bed for weeks at a time.

Multiple sclerosis is a progressive neurological illness with no cure. Although my symptoms became more frequent and severe, at least I could still live independently. A sense of humor helped me cope with everything. My memory was so bad that many times I had to resort to charades. At first, it was devastating not to know something simple, like a broom. I remember the first time I had to act out what I was trying to communicate.

"I need that thing that is on a stick. When you hold it, you do this" (which was me mimicking sweeping because at that point, besides the word *broom*, I also could not remember the word *sweep*).

Most of my friends accepted my difficulties. My son could tell just by looking at me how I was doing. If he thought I was overdoing it, he would gently suggest taking a nap.

I found it interesting that as I lost the ability for my brain to function well with left-brain activities, it compensated by increasing my abilities to use the more artistic right side of the brain. When I would work on a creative project, it didn't affect me in the same way. It didn't seem to take as much out of me if it was only a creative project.

My life continued to be drastically changed with multiple sclerosis. Fortunately, these enormous challenges brought me back to my spiritual path in a big way. When you have something this devastating, it is comforting and empowering to connect with your spiritual life. I felt the MS was in my body to bring lessons to me; I trusted that whatever Spirit had planned for me was fine. I would accept and deal with it if I had it for the rest of this lifetime. My goal was to tackle and understand whatever lessons MS was bringing to me.

Chapter 4
Digging Deeper

After three years of Florida heat aggravating the MS, and causing me to be homebound, I moved to the beautiful mountain town of Asheville, North Carolina. It took me a while to realize Spirit orchestrated my move there to fast-track my spiritual journey. It brought me to a much deeper understanding of how so many things in our lives are not just random coincidences. If I didn't have MS, I might have never moved to Asheville. This move reignited my entire spiritual world.

After my arrival, I attended the opening ceremony of the Loving Kindness Tour of the ancient Buddhist Relics exhibit. The monks and volunteers hosting the event filled the night with chanting, prayer, and meditation. Many people have experienced mystical power transmissions and healing after witnessing these sacred relics.

I also received Shaktipat from one of the Buddhist monks, which is a direct transmission of spiritual energy to awaken higher states of consciousness. He said prayers and gently touched my third eye chakra, blessing me with the powerful initiation energy. This chakra sits between the eyebrows and focuses on clairvoyance, visions, intuition, wisdom, and extrasensory perceptions.

Soon after the Shaktipat and the Buddhist Ancient Relic exhibit, I had a spontaneous Kundalini awakening as I listened to some powerful sacred drumming music.

Many spiritual traditions believe Kundalini is a unique energy source coiled like a snake at the base of your spine. As Kundalini energy moves through the body, the chakra energy centers activate and align, clearing energetic blockages. A Kundalini awakening is about transformation, shedding our old ways for an enlightened life.

My Kundalini awakening was an unexpected, phenomenal experience. Blissful sensations filled and surrounded my body. Energy flowed throughout my chakra energy centers. It felt like each chakra was having mind-blowing orgasms. My creativity, spiritual insights, and awareness increased exponentially. I embraced my increased inspiration, love, wisdom, and enhanced intuition; my entire being was overflowing with Divine love and light!

After the spontaneous Kundalini awakening, all my senses remained heightened. My healing and psychic abilities, visions, dreams, out-of-body experiences, and creativity were all enhanced. Spontaneous orgasms became a regular occurrence. Snakes began showing up in my dreams and the physical world. Twice I had poisonous copperheads appear at the front door of my house, coiled and ready to strike. I lost count of how many snakes I saw in my dreams.

I didn't fully appreciate the significance and impact of witnessing the ancient Buddhist relics, receiving Shaktipat, and the spontaneous Kundalini awakening all happening so closely together. Only now do I realize their connection to my unexpected visits with two medical intuitives, who use their intuition to scan the body to check if anything is out of balance. They both noted a trauma from early childhood had remained in my body.

Insights from medical intuitives

Does it seem far-fetched that a person can diagnose a medical problem just by feeling your energy and checking in with their intuition? I was slightly skeptical when I first heard about medical intuitives. If I suspected I broke my arm, would I have an X-ray or would I check in with a medical intuitive? Although my first choice is usually alternative healing, I also respect there is a time and place for Western medicine. I want X-rays and a good orthopedic doctor for a possible broken bone.

Twice, in my mid-fifties, I unwittingly had sessions with medical intuitives. While working on me, a physical therapist stopped when she got to my right lower calf.

"What happened to you when you were three years old?"

"I don't know. I think that's when my parents divorced. Why are you asking?"

"Something traumatic happened to you at that age that is still locked in your body."

I answered, "I am sure a divorce at that age seemed very traumatic."

She replied, "I encourage you to find out if there was any other trauma."

A few months later, I hired a massage therapist. As my entire body settled into a deeply relaxed state, my attention jolted back to the room.

She asked me the same question when she began working on my lower right calf.

"What happened to you when you were three years old?"

Not knowing how else to respond, I gave her the same answer, "I think that is when my parents got divorced."

But this time, I couldn't shake it. Two different professionals, who were also medical intuitives, had observed the same energy in my right calf. I dug deeper, determined to find out if something else happened to me other than my parent's divorce.

I had heard that Dr. Shannon South uses a unique process to identify and heal traumatic events. Shannon is an expert in mind-body-spirit and trauma healing. As an award-winning transpersonal therapist, she taps into your spiritual nature and deeper knowing during her sessions. She incorporates guided meditation, visualization, and mindfulness techniques to overcome trauma and issues like anxiety, depression, stress, and panic attacks.

Shannon practices what she preaches. Almost thirty years ago, while in graduate school, she had a spiritual epiphany that healed her debilitating anxiety and panic attacks.

Our session began with Shannon asking what brought me to see her. After I told her what the two medical intuitives had said, she asked me to close my eyes. Her process begins with finding a relaxing place. My auspicious place was a cliff overlooking an ocean with a large tree where I could sit and enjoy the view while listening to the waves crash.

"Is there anyone else with you?"

"This is interesting. Some of my close friends and my son have joined me."

Then Shannon urged me to relax and go deeper. She guided me to a time when I was three years old.

"What do you see?"

"My parents are fighting. My father is drunk."

"What are they fighting about?"

With my heart racing and my hands clammy, a floodgate of tears opened.

"What is happening?"

All I could do was cry. I couldn't form any words. I was in shock.

Shannon waited until my cries were quiet.

"I can't believe this is happening! When I was a teenager, someone told me about a time when my dad was drunk and had a gun, threatening to kill my mother. I remember expressing how grateful l was that I did not experience it."

"Can you tell me what you are seeing?"

Sobbing, I could barely speak.

I answered, "My dad has a gun in the middle of my forehead. I can feel the cold barrel right between my eyes."

"Oh my God! He just cocked the gun! I am going to die! I am only three years old, and my dad is going to kill all of us, starting with me. He picked me as the first one to kill, even though I thought I was his favorite."

Back in that moment, frozen in time, it was too traumatic to continue looking at the event. Shannon brought me back so we could talk about it.

Shell-shocked, I had little strength to continue. At least my dad didn't shoot any of us; we all were still alive. This had been such a traumatic event that I buried it from myself for over fifty years. I experienced anger and disappointment with my mother for not leaving my dad sooner. He had been an out-of-control alcoholic and rage addict during their entire marriage.

My mother did not have the inner strength to leave my dad until he threatened to kill me and the rest of the family with a gun. I don't think I ever fully regained respect for her after that happened. The event scared my dad sober. All these years, I was told he became sober when I turned three. Now I realize his sobriety hinged on this deplorable event.

I am still in awe of how the two medical intuitives could sense something significant happened to me when I was three, just by holding my right calf. Alternative healing asks us to go outside of our comfort zone, to stretch our minds to be open to additional information and possibilities. It is all about learning to surrender and trust. Spiritual healing reveals things when you are ready.

So much made sense after this session with Shannon. I understood why I had a troublesome time respecting my mother. My family kept the incident an enormous secret. No wonder after my parents divorced, I didn't want to go visit my dad. My mother forced me to go. At three years old, I knew what was happening in my life was not okay or safe.

Over fifty years later, I see it as a big lesson about life not always being fair. It also gave me clarity about trusting my intuition. My sweet, innocent little three-year-old self knew I was living in an unstable and crazy environment.

The medical intuitives' insights and Shannon's session confirmed that I had been right about my family. I could now go back and empower my little three-year-old self, thanking her for her strength and bravery—for helping me to survive, thrive, and protect me until I was strong enough to acknowledge what happened.

We all inherently "know" what is true and just. Our intuition is here to protect and guide us. Spirit reveals more when we are ready.

These events—the Buddhist Relics exhibit, receiving Shaktipat, the spontaneous Kundalini awakening, the message from the two medical intuitives—all helped to clear the trauma I had been harboring for over fifty years. I experienced a deeper remembering and recovery of my authentic spiritual self, embracing my Divine path. For the next several years, I was on a warp-speed trajectory.

Chapter 5

Remembering How to Heal Others

———— ༄༅༅ ————

In 2009, I told Spirit I wanted to share my energy healing with others. The next day, a friend came to visit. When I opened the door, he had a book in his hand.

"I was already in my car when something told me to go back inside my house and get this book. I don't know why, but I think I am supposed to give it to you."

As he handed me the book, it amazed me to see that it was about energy healing work.

Later that night, when I took a long relaxing soak in my clawfoot bathtub, I began reading the book. Before I finished the first chapter, messages and specific guidance for healing started coming to me. It turned out to be my introduction to the Spirit Guides, who would help me do energetic healing work on other people.

I had a close friend with kidney stone problems. In a great deal of pain, she was trying to wait until she qualified for insurance at her new job to have the stone removed. I offered to do some remote healing work for her. She agreed because the persistent pain had become almost unbearable.

What an amazing experience! My Spirit Guides assisted me the entire time, telling me what to do. The results relieved my friend of her immediate pain. After a week, her pain returned since she had not yet expelled the stone. I suggested trying another session to get her pain-free until her insurance would cover having the stone removed. By then, her pain was excruciating, requiring several trips to the emergency room. My guides gave me different instructions for her next healing session, and she remained free of pain until the first day her insurance became active, which had been our goal.

I performed my next healing on a medical doctor. I met him at a Reiki Tummo training. Reiki Tummo is a specific type of energy healing that uses symbols and other techniques. Reiki originated in Japan, and means "vital energy"; *tummo* is the Tibetan word for "inner fire" which refers to Kundalini energy. Reiki uses Divine energy to heal. Reiki Tummo includes all the benefits of traditional Reiki, plus a more heart-centered approach to healing, and a focus on awakening the Kundalini.

I thought it seemed like a good idea to get more training. It didn't take me long to realize if I adhered to someone else's ideas, processes, and techniques for doing healing work, I could not heed my Spirit Guides. During a break at the training, the doctor and I talked. He asked me what I thought about the training.

"I am a bit confused and conflicted. If I try to focus on using all the details of Reiki, I can't hear my Spirit Guides."

He asked me about the type of energy healing I do. When I told him what happened with my friend and the pain with her kidney stone, his response surprised me.

"What you did for your friend is amazing. I know how painful kidney stones can be for people. In that situation, doctors may give the patient something like morphine for pain, but the relief does not last after the medicine wears off. You have an extraordinary gift. I think you need to stick with your guides and not worry about getting other training."

As we continued talking, I told him I had only done remote healings. He offered to let me work on his injured leg. Admittedly, I was a little nervous about working on him because he was a medical doctor. My Spirit Guides did not let me down.

Several guides showed up as soon as I began working on him. I could see them sitting across the table from me. The first one to appear was a Native American chief. Then an Irishman showed up. The last to join us was an older woman, who I assumed was the doctor's grandmother. Since I had never had Spirit Guides appear in a physical body form, I thought these were all the doctor's guides who came to help with his healing.

After I finished the healing, I told him, "Three of your Spirit Guides were here." As I described them, he affirmed the older woman must have been his grandmother. The other two didn't resonate with him.

He told me, "Thank you so much for your healing. I am super relaxed, and my leg feels better. I can't wait to try it out on an extended bicycle ride."

My second in-person healing was with an older woman struggling with pain for quite some time. She had never experienced energy healing work.

She told me, "I have tried so many things to get some relief from this back pain. I am desperate and will try almost anything."

As I worked on her, I looked up—there was the Native American chief and the Irishman. This time the chief took part in the healing. So, they weren't the doctor's guides after all—they were mine, here to help me with my healing work.

My client shared what she experienced during the session.

"I am very relaxed, and the pain is much less severe." She continued, "I didn't tell you, but I told my husband before I scheduled my appointment with you that maybe a Native American healing would help."

I responded, "That's outstanding because a Native American chief helped me work on you today."

After these first two in-person healings, the Irishman and the Native American chief did not come to any more of my healings. Some Spirit Guides show up a few times, do their work, and never return. However, the energy of the Native American chief appeared during a shamanic drumming journey ten years later, when I lived in San Miguel de Allende, Mexico.

Chapter 6
Guided Past Life Regression

———— ༄༅༆ ————

After moving to Asheville, North Carolina, I had an extraordinary encounter with a neighbor. Micah and I were talking outside my house. As he moved closer to me, I inhaled his breath; in an instant, memories flashed in my mind. It was like watching a movie of my life at warp speed. It rebooted my entire spiritual existence.

"I remember you. I recognize your soul. This is much more than just recalling a past life. I have known you forever," I said as I looked into Micah's eyes.

Later, we observed our faces shape-shift into four distinct faces, representing our different lifetimes together. Micah considered me a seer, one who sees the world through spiritual eyes and can foresee and interpret Divine truth.

I wanted to understand in more depth why Micah had crossed my path, so I scheduled a past life regression therapy session with John Williams, M.Ed., C.Ht. Although I can recall past lives, sometimes I use a past life regression therapist to assist with my own past life journeys. John uses a gentle form of hypnotherapy to help you uncover your past.

After John took some notes on my purpose and intentions for the session, we moved into the treatment room. I lay down on a massage table and closed my eyes. He played some relaxing music and led me in a guided meditation.

As I became more relaxed, he took me back in time. First, John had me remember some things that happened in this lifetime. He continued until we reached my early childhood. Then we crossed over into past lives.

"Tell me when you move beyond this lifetime."

I responded, "I am somewhere else."

"Where are you?"

"I'm not sure."

"Glance down at your feet. What shoes are you wearing?"

"I have on sandals. Wow! It looks like I am in Greece. I am standing on the steps of a temple holding my baby, who I recognize is my current son. Micah is my husband. He is standing next to me, with his arm wrapped around my shoulder."

I paused.

"What is happening?" John asked.

I hesitated. It was difficult getting the words out.

"We are all dead. Micah and I were the leaders of our community. There was a coup; they killed us."

"Is there anything else from this life you want to see?"

"No, I'm good."

"Is there another life you would like to visit?"

"I am receiving information about why we came to this planet. They sent us here to bring an ancient healing technique."

"What is the name of the healing?" John asked.

"The words Yin Yang healing are coming to me," I responded.

"Where are you?" John asked.

"I am at the Source Planet. The Wise Ones' leaders sent us to Egypt to bring the Yin Yang healing."

"Where is the Source Planet?"

"It is in another dimension."

"Who are the Wise Ones?"

"They are some of the wisest and most powerful beings in the Universe. The Wise Ones are the only ones that can do the Yin Yang Healing, which is a potent method of energy healing."

"Can you do the Yin Yang healing?"

"Not anymore. I think something bad happened in Egypt."

"Is there anything else you want to look at today?"

"No, I am good. I think we covered enough for today. I will sit with all of this and see what comes up later."

Meeting people from ancient Egypt

After the past life regression, I began meeting people from that Egyptian lifetime. Most of them I recognized. I would start by asking, "Do you have any memories or feelings about Egypt?"

As we shared thoughts, feelings, and memories, pieces of the puzzle about that Egyptian lifetime started coming together.

My spiritual awareness and abilities increased after I started having the Egyptian memories. Someone would talk, and my Spirit Guides would tell me to ask the person to repeat themselves. After repeating the same words several times, in the same way, visions would appear. I had experienced prophetic visions and dreams for years, but never while wide awake.

Micah's Soul Body began visiting me. I could perceive him with all my senses. Sometimes he came just to hang out with me; other times, it was to help me. I had never experienced this before, and at first thought perhaps it was just my imagination.

In the beginning, his Soul Body visited me several times a week at my house. What convinced me it was not my imagination was when Micah's Soul Body appeared at my dental appointment. I have always experienced anxiety when I go to the dentist. As I sat in the dental chair with my mouth wide open and my eyes shut, I felt someone cradling my hand. It surprised me to realize it was Micah's Soul Body.

"What are you doing here?" I asked him.

"I wanted to be here with you because I know how nervous you get at the dentist's office," Micah replied.

Since I saw Bob, a psychic healer, right after my dental appointment, we discussed what had been happening with Micah.

"Am I imagining this, or is his Soul Body showing up?" I asked.

Bob had me lie on his table for an assessment and healing. He read my body and spirit and then performed energy work on me.

"Yes, Chloe, Micah's soul has been visiting you. And yes, that was him at the dentist's office."

Later, I asked Micah if he had any awareness of visiting me spiritually.

"No, I didn't realize that was happening. But it's pretty cool, isn't it?"

That's when I came up with the name "Soul Body." Micah and I have had an intense soul connection from our first life together. When Micah came to visit me with his Soul Body, it was not Micah in the third dimension (3D) physical world that made that happen. It was his soul who appeared in an ethereal body that I could see, hear, touch, and feel. A Soul Body can astral travel without the 3D person realizing it.

The most significant time Micah's Soul Body came to me was on 11/11/11, the first time those three numbers aligned in a hundred years. In numerology and astrology, the number 11 signifies a connection to your inner self, intuition, and spiritual awakening.

That night, I did a spiritual journey on my BETAR sound vibration chakra table. It looks like a massage table. Underneath the padded area where you lie, ten speakers are placed to reach your main energy points. The BETAR connects to a CD player and a headset speaker. This allows you to hear the music and receive the vibration sound on a cellular level throughout your body. Think of it as a super-charged, relaxing "musical massage" that can aid healing and spiritual awakening.

As I lay on the table, I started experiencing a spontaneous pineal gland activation. At that moment, Micah's Soul Body arrived. He took my hand and told me not to worry, that he would stay with me until the activation was completed.

Before going deeper with the pineal activation, I remembered a sound healing experience I had with Micah. He told me I surrendered to the process so deeply that he feared I would not come back to my body. Micah warned me not to do deep journeys by myself. I then understood why he came to help me through the activation; I relaxed and surrendered to the experience.

After Micah's Soul Body left, my Spirit Guides shared this poignant message with me:

"Just because somebody may have been a deeply spiritual, awakened being in a past life doesn't mean they will always be that way in other lives. I understand how close you are to Micah's soul; don't let that confuse you about who he is and how he is living his life now. In this lifetime, Micah can only hold a sacred space in the 3D world for a limited time."

The third dimension focuses on the physical world, with its limitations, fear, and suffering. If you are only accessing the 3D world, it is like being locked into that view of time and space; it affects your ability to grow spiritually.

That Spirit Guide message resonated with me. A friend had mentioned to me before that she noticed I can connect directly with other people's souls.

She said, "When you connect in that way, their soul responds to your soul. But, it is not a space they, in their 3D bodies, can hold for long periods of time. It is almost like you are bypassing the 3D person to connect with their soul."

Another similar experience I had during this time was when my son's Soul Body came to visit me. I was staying at a remote cabin in the Smoky Mountains. My son was not aware I was there. One night around 3 a.m., I woke up, startled to observe my son's Soul Body standing in the doorway.

I asked him, "What are you doing here? How did you know where to find me?"

He answered, "The Big One told me to come here."

My immediate thought was that the Big One was God.

I thought, "Cool, sent by God; can't get much better than that!"

However, when I tried to fall back to sleep, I worried that maybe my son had died, and that's why God told him to come to the cabin. My cell phone didn't work at the cabin, so I had no way of finding out if my son had called my house in Asheville.

When I returned home later that morning, my heart started pounding when I saw I had a phone message from my son. He called at 3 a.m., the exact time his Soul Body showed up at my cabin.

"Hey, Mom, sorry to call you so late. I have been staying with friends. We went out tonight, and when we came back, we realized someone had robbed their house. They stole everything of value that I own. I am done; I need to get out of this town and settle down somewhere new. Would you be willing to help me come to Asheville?"

Within a few weeks, my son moved to Asheville.

Chapter 7

Visions: 2010–2011

My vision dreams became more detailed and frequent during these intense years of spiritual growth and awareness. Some were prophetic dreams about the future. Others were memories of past lives. I also had dreams of living in parallel lives.

One particular prophetic dream alarmed me, so I contacted a dream interpreter. Her response shocked me.

"There are people all over the country having this dream right now. Not everything in the dreams is the same, but they all have the same three key components."

1. a "natural" disaster
2. martial law
3. microchipping by the government

When many people have very similar prophetic dreams, I pay attention. It means we were all experiencing collective energy.

If you heard about only one person having that dream, it might sound like an interesting dream, but perhaps not likely to happen. When multiple people all over the country are having the dream simultaneously, how can that be a coincidence? We are tapping into collective energy and information. Hearing about all the people who had this dream during the same period is significant. None of us knew each other, yet our dreams all reflected the same type of event.

During this time, I had a series of waking visions and prophetic dreams that focused on the aftermath of a worldwide disaster and rebuilding our planet. My Spirit Guides told me they would give us extraordinary gifts that would protect us and enhance our healing abilities.

My most intense vision dream was the one that many people were having at the same time. In the dream, I was walking in the center of town with a friend. In the blink of an eye, buildings and people disappeared. Turning to look behind me, I noticed a huge tsunami of fire. Hoping to find a safe place, I ran toward a building that was still standing.

Upon entering, I noticed snakes everywhere. They slithered and coiled between the few remaining structures that resembled sacred artifacts among what remained of the building. I saw another doorway at the end of the building. As I got closer, I observed a huge cobra guarding the door. For a second, this twenty-foot venomous king cobra serpent frightened me. A sense of peace and safety washed over me as I remembered, "Of course. The king cobra is the gatekeeper."

As I walked past the cobra, it surprised me to find a room intact with twelve people sitting around a coffee table. Still in shock, everyone was trying to piece together what had happened. I recognized an old-fashioned black phone with a rotary dial hanging on the wall. I grabbed the receiver, relieved to hear a dial tone.

"Hey, guys. This phone is working!" I exclaimed.

The group decided each person could make one brief phone call. Halfway through the calls, I overheard some commotion outside.

I exclaimed, "Oh, no! It's the military."

Most of the group was excited, thinking the military would help us.

I responded, "Be careful. Things are not always as they seem. I don't think their true intention is to help. Please be quiet, so they don't realize we are here."

Some of our group ran out of the room, yelling and waving at the military procession. A few of the military personnel came into the room.

"Don't worry. We are here to help. You all will be okay. We are taking everyone to a center where you will have a place to stay and food to eat."

I did not want to go. They insisted everyone had to vacate the building and come with them. They had gathered a large group of people, herding everyone like cattle toward what resembled a toll booth. Each person had something injected into their arm before they could move through the turnstile.

"What are they putting in each person's arm?" I asked the military personnel.

"It's just a vaccine to protect you," he responded.

"Protect us from what?"

He ignored my question and hurried away.

"Oh my God," I whispered to the person standing next to me. "They are microchipping everyone. Once they chip you, the game's over. They will use it to track everything you do. I would rather die trying to escape than submit to what they have planned for us. I have a cabin in the mountains. Let's make a run for it."

I am convinced it was not just a coincidence that random people all over the country were all dreaming about a natural disaster, martial law, and microchipping at the same time.

Parallel universe and dreams

The quantum physics theory of the multiverse includes the concept of a parallel universe. It takes seriously the possibility of other universes. A parallel universe is where your life can play out in other realities.

One of my most disturbing dreams appeared in a parallel universe. In the dream, I was in a New Orleans-style shotgun house that seemed familiar, like I had lived there. When I got to the back end of the house, I opened the door to a pitch-black room. There was a bed next to me. Exhausted, I lay down.

After a short while, I realized there was another bed in the room, and something was in that bed. Dark energy was emanating from the other bed. Since I am a lucid dreamer, I could pause the dream for a second to assess the situation. I felt a strong need to let the dream continue, so I cautiously reentered the dream.

I saw that a masculine entity was now sitting on the other bed in a long black hooded cloak. As he stood, my entire body tensed up. An acute sense of impending doom filled the room. What happened next was not just a dream but happening in a parallel life.

The cloaked being reached into his pocket and pulled out a matchbox. Then he pulled out a match and placed it on the striking area of the matchbox. I knew if the match ignited, it would burn me.

As he walked toward me, I forced myself to wake up. Unlike most dreams that dissipate after you awake, I could still see the entity trying to reach me. Instinctively, I raised my hands toward the heavens and prayed.

"I am from the Light. You must leave." I repeated it over and over.

What happened the next day stunned me. I was sitting on my porch, telling a friend about the dream. When I got to the part about the being walking toward me, ready to light the match, my friend interrupted me.

"Chloe, don't you remember what I taught you many lifetimes ago? When you are in danger, you need to point your hands toward the heavens and say, I am from the Light. You must leave."

Astonished, I blurted, "What?! That is exactly what I did last night!"

My friend responded, "Chloe, they assigned me to protect you many lifetimes ago. I have been following you for as long as I can remember. It is my responsibility to keep you safe."

Chapter 8

More Clarity: 2012

———— ⌐⌐⌐ ————

A woman who had lived and trained with shamans in Peru for twelve years came to visit Asheville. Highly respected shamans are the healers and advisors of their community. Among their gifts are the ability to manipulate reality, divination, forecast future outcomes, and heal physical, mental, emotional, and spiritual issues. They can access and communicate with other dimensions, animals, plants, and the spirit world.

I booked an appointment, hoping to get some answers and clarity from her about my visions and newfound abilities. I told her about my ability to experience people's past lives. She asked me to tell her everything I do during my energy healing sessions.

"I want to know what happens, from the moment someone knocks on your door until they leave."

"First, I clear their energy. Then I give them a brief explanation of what to expect during the session, making sure they understand Spirit Guides direct me on what to do. I mention the more they can relax and surrender to the process, the deeper we can go.

"Before having them lie down, we set intentions for their session. After they get on the table, I place stones on each of the major chakra points and have them close their eyes. My Spirit Guides help me select music that will accommodate the intentions of the session. Then I sit, close my eyes, and go into a trance.

"Once I am in the trance state, I place my hands on different parts of their body, based on the instructions from my Spirit Guides. If Spirit has information about a past life, I get sensations and visions. It is like I am viewing a movie, and can witness people, places, and things that happened in their past life.

"It usually involves their death, which I re-experience for them so that anything that got stuck from their death in that lifetime gets released. The past life memories that I recall are challenging for me, as I am not only seeing them, but also experiencing all the original emotions and sensations the person had during their death.

"The last step is processing what happened during the session.

"First, I ask how the session was for them. Then I ask if they would like to know what I experienced. We talk until they have a good understanding of the session."

In deep contemplative thought, the shaman broke her silence.

"You are one of us."

"What do you mean, one of us?" I asked.

"It is clear you have done shamanic work in other lifetimes. Most of us forget and need to retrain. They blessed you with the ability to tap in and remember your training.

"It's all connected—your energy healing work, the visions, seeing and interacting with Soul Bodies, collective dreaming, recalling past lives, your awareness of parallel universes, and your deep connection to your Spirit Guides."

This was not the first time someone had told me I was a shaman. A few years earlier, I was outside on my deck with a friend. With my eyes closed, I prayed and called in energy with my hands. When I opened my eyes, my friend was staring at me.

"Chloe, you are a shaman," he announced.

"No, I'm not," I responded. "Why are you saying that?"

"Because you lit up the entire neighborhood just by moving your hands and your arms. Do you realize how powerful you are?"

An unexpected connection

In November 2012, a friend and I attended a drumming class led by world-renowned musician, composer, educator, and sound immersion healer River Guerguerian. He has had a successful career, working with Grammy and Oscar winners; playing concerts all over the world; recording over 250 albums and film tracks; and performing with the BBC Symphony Orchestra, Paul Winter Consort, Chuck Berry, Ziggy Marley, the Gipsy Kings, and other well-known musicians.

One of my favorite things about River is that he got rid of all his possessions and lived off-grid in a Himalayan wildlife sanctuary for five years. This inspired his interest in the physiological effects of sound. My guess is that his time there also significantly impacted River's sound immersion healing therapy.

That night, River finished the class with an amazing sound immersion session. He had everyone lie on the floor and close their eyes. River walked around and played different percussion instruments over everyone's bodies. To hear and experience the instrument's vibrations on your body is an amazing experience!

Afterward, I had a strong sense that River and I would work together on some projects. I walked over to him, introduced myself, thanked him for the class and sound immersion. Then I told him I would like him to do a community sound immersion on 12/12/12, an auspicious date for increased spiritual growth.

River didn't miss a beat.

"Okay. If you take care of the marketing, I'll do it."

"Fantastic! Marketing is my specialty. Thank you."

The first event sold out in less than a day. We added a second session, which was also full within a day.

After the 12/12/12 event, I approached River and said I thought we should organize a larger gathering on 12/21/12, another significant spiritual date. Again, with no hesitation, he agreed to do it. River found the space and convinced several of his musician friends to participate in this free community event.

The evening closed with an amazing sound immersion by River and some of the other musicians. I went so deep that after it was over, I wasn't certain if I had been there for five minutes, five weeks, five months, or five years.

It seemed so far out; I didn't mention it to anyone. As I was helping clean up, River came into the cafeteria area and asked if anyone had experienced a time vortex opening. I was the only one to respond.

"Thank goodness I wasn't the only one to notice the shift in time."

Since working with River, I noticed when our energies connect, vortexes open. After realizing that River had also felt a time dimension open that night, I knew I didn't imagine it.

Chapter 9

2013: Old Challenges and New Beginnings

———— ༄༅༆ ————

A music producer friend suggested River and I try to capture our combined energy on a recording.

I told River, "I noticed something powerful and profound happens when we combine our energy. Let's mic up my body and record you doing a sound immersion on me so we can capture our combined energy."

Two days before the recording, my Spirit Guides told me the Wise Ones wanted to be on the recording. The next day I did a past life regression to check in with the Wise Ones. I told them I did not know how to bring them to the recording. They told me everything would work out.

"Don't worry. We will take care of everything."

On the day of the recording, River and I said a prayer and sealed it with our intention of capturing our combined energies with the Wise Ones.

I lay on my back, resting on the sacred blankets River uses for his private sound immersion healing sessions. After he placed microphones on different parts of my body, he started playing an array of percussion instruments on and around my body. For this session, River used drums, cymbals, singing bowls, gongs, chimes, marimba, and shakers. His sound immersion sessions are both powerful and relaxing. I wondered if I would recognize the Wise Ones' presence.

River checked the recording after the sound immersion ended.

"I am so sorry. Not everything was recorded. Would you mind coming back tomorrow morning to do it again?"

Since I was uncertain if the Wise Ones were on the first recording, it relieved me to do another recording.

The next morning was a Saturday. River and I were the only people in the building besides the janitor. The minute River began the sound immersion; I started having roller-coaster / tilt-a-whirl sensations, starting with my belly and continuing throughout my body. My heart started beating faster. I felt weightless as if floating. It filled my body and mind with sensations of euphoria. I was in the most naturally altered state I had ever experienced.

I trust the Wise Ones, so I took a deep breath and surrendered to the journey. They did not leave until the sound immersion was over. River checked the recording. We were both thrilled with the results.

River and I express ourselves differently. I am primarily extroverted, talkative, and enthusiastic. River is much more laid-back and quiet. We are the epitome of yin and yang. Whereas I might bubble over with excitement, River remains calm and cool.

Yin and yang are about duality, and how those differences can be complementary and interconnected. It's like fitting pieces into a puzzle to make a whole. When River and I are together—combining our energies—pieces come together, and vortexes and other dimensions open. Our ability to combine our efforts and unlock energy opens an entire plethora of opportunities.

My way of expressing my feelings about the sound healing that morning was unbridled enthusiasm. River was much more subdued. Picture the ultra-cool jazz legend Miles Davis—strong yet vulnerable, taking everything in, but not always needing to comment. I am more of a Janis Joplin vibe—raw, intense, impassioned.

River commented, "I think we got it this time."

I commented, "Oh my God! The Wise Ones were here! Their energy swirled around and in me from the first moment you began playing your instruments. They remained until the end. This is going to be an amazing recording!"

One day, when we were editing the recording together in River's studio, I started experiencing flashes of past lives River and I have had together. We were healers in many lives. The most significant connection was the lifetime in ancient Egypt with the Yin Yang healing.

"Of course," I thought. "River was part of the group that came from the Wise Ones' planet to Egypt. No wonder the Wise Ones gave their blessing to be a part of this recording."

A connection to the past

Later in 2013, I had an extraordinary healing experience. During my annual physical, my doctor told me she found a large lump in my right breast. I thought she was kidding since I had told her I wasn't sure I wanted annual mammograms anymore because of the radiation exposure.

"So, if there seemed to be a problem, would you have a mammogram? This is not a joke. Let me have your hand so you can feel it yourself," she said.

After I left the doctor's office, my goal was to make the lump disappear before we got to the biopsy stage. As I was making my list of alternative healers I wanted to use, I remembered that Bob, my psychic healer, had told me years ago he saw cancer energy around my right breast.

"It is not in your breast yet. I want you to be aware of it, so hopefully, you can prevent it from spreading to your body."

Bob was the first healer I called about the lump in my breast my doctor had found. As a psychic medium and healer, he can remove unwanted spirits and energy, contact people who have crossed over, communicate with nature and animals, and perform psychic readings to help you with decisions.

I told him, "Well, I have good news and bad news. The good news is that you are an amazing psychic. At least five years ago, you told me that I had cancer energy circling my right breast. Today my doctor found a large lump in my right breast." I continued, "And the bad news is that now I may have breast cancer."

Bob connected with his Spirit guides. They had a lot to say.

"First, I need you to accept this is serious. There is cancer in the right breast. Before I continue, I need you to agree that you will not postpone any medical care. There is no time to first explore alternative healing solutions. You must keep all appointments with your traditional medical doctors. Alternative solutions are fine as long as you continue to follow the Western medical options as well."

He continued, "My guides are saying one of your grandmothers wants to help you remove the cancer."

"Oh, I bet it is my Gran Mamie. We were close."

Bob said no, it was my maternal grandmother, which surprised me. During this lifetime, she didn't seem like someone who would show up in the afterlife to help with healing.

"All you need to do is allow her to help. She wants to do this for you."

I was staying in a remote cabin in the mountains. Bob suggested I go out in nature.

"There is a large tree outside that can help with your healing. Find it and let it know you are ready to receive its healing energy."

I went to one of my favorite trees that overlooked a little creek.

"Thank you, dear wise tree, for agreeing to help heal me. I am open, ready, and grateful to receive your powerful healing energy."

The next morning I had my breast ultrasound. I had booked appointments with two other healers after the ultrasound. If the doctor ordered a biopsy, I wanted more healing work before having it done.

After the ultrasound, a doctor came in to discuss the results.

"Your breasts look fine. I don't see any lumps in either breast."

Amazed that the lump had disappeared, I still kept the two other healing appointments to ensure the cancer would not come back.

When I arrived at River's studio, I told him the good news.

River asked, "Do you remember when I first met you last year? I asked if you had cancer?"

"Yes, I do," I replied. "I thought you were asking me because you work with a lot of cancer patients."

"No. I asked you because I saw cancer in your right breast. When you assured me you had never had cancer, I thought maybe my vision was wrong."

River did an amazing sound immersion healing on me. His healing abilities had increased since the session we recorded with the Wise Ones.

My next appointment was with Dr. Shannon South, the holistic transpersonal therapist. Holistic healing encompasses the whole person, considering physical, mental, social, and spiritual factors. Shannon's mystical process connects with your Spirit Guides to help look at what your current situation is trying to tell you. Every time I do this process with Shannon, the wisdom, guidance, and healing are so potent. It's astonishing what one session can accomplish.

Even with all the miraculous healing news, a friend of mine encouraged me to go back to the doctor who found the lump for her to confirm she could no longer feel it.

"I can't find the lump. I have never seen a lump that size disappear in a matter of days. You are very lucky."

I knew my alternative healing experiences would sound woo-woo to her, so I just smiled and nodded my head.

Chapter 10

2014–2016: Sometimes You May Need a Spiritual Break

———— ༃ႶᏊ ————

Spiritual work can seem too intense and overwhelming at times. Twice in my life, I had to take a break. In my early thirties, I had extreme spiritual experiences that were far out, even for me. One night, I started levitating. At first, I thought I was just dreaming. I opened my eyes and saw my entire body suspended several feet above my bed.

My move to Asheville reignited my spiritual life, propelling me into a warp-speed initiation. While it was exciting and rewarding to reawaken so quickly, it was also intense. I never knew when a waking vision would show up. Most of the time, I would be in the middle of a conversation when the awake visions would appear.

Even the prophetic dreams became exhausting. They were frequent; I felt a tremendous responsibility to pay attention to all the visions. My visions never gave me a date, so each time, I would wonder, "Is this going to be happening soon?" It was like I was always on call.

Some visions were heartbreaking. It is very challenging to be aware of future problems and not know if you can do anything to change the outcome. Sometimes I wondered why they showed me so many visions of the future if they didn't want me to help heal and improve it.

I remember a detailed prophetic dream and subsequent conversation I had with my Spirit Guides. In this dream, our planet was being rescued and rebuilt by beings from another dimension. At first, elated that help would come, I started questioning why they weren't willing to come earlier. As a "make it happen" person all my life, it was challenging to have all these problematic visions and not know if I could help alter the future course.

I asked my guides, "If you are planning on coming to save our planet, why are you waiting? Based on my visions, there is going to be so much suffering!"

"We know. But, we can't come yet. We have to wait for as many people as possible to wake up with their own free will."

I understood their point, yet I still found it distressing that so many people would suffer before things changed.

My encounter with a Walk-In

One night before asking Spirit to let me take a break, I met a man who thought he was a Walk-In. Many believe that another soul can enter a body as a Walk-In if the original soul agrees. This man said he remembered being from another planet and had crashed his spaceship. They gave him the opportunity to be a Walk-In, so he accepted the offer.

He was aware of many things I had been seeing. In some of our visions, we saw trains filled with people going in different directions. The ones who "woke up" were going one way; the others who had refused to awaken were going in a different direction.

By 2014, all the visions and spiritual experiences I had for the past six years exhausted me. I wanted some time without the responsibility of having so many spiritual visions and insights. I asked Spirit to please let me take a break.

For around three years, I lived a normal life. No more recognizing people from the Egyptian lifetime. No more alarming dreaming or waking visions. Micah's Soul Body did not appear anymore. Just quiet peace and contentment.

Creativity and the sacral chakra

During my spiritual break, I used the time to focus on my creativity, which is connected to the sacral second chakra, below your belly button. I had inherited a mannequin that was pulled from the rubble of the Oklahoma City bombing and had not figured out what type of art project I could do to honor the people who perished. They found the mannequin on the first floor of the Federal Building, wedged between a xerox machine, with a bathing suit covering half of its body. I named the mannequin Molly and put her in my living room so I would see her all the time.

After the mannequin had been standing in my living room for almost a year, a friend stopped by my house to walk over to the West Asheville Yoga Studio. We were attending an evening of kirtan, a Vedic tradition that uses songs and chants in a call and response style to get in touch with the Divine.

My friend noticed the mannequin and asked me if I had decided what to do with it.

"I am still not sure. I keep her in the living room, hoping to receive some inspiration and direction."

Once the kirtan music began, I relaxed into a trance state. The music performed by Sean Jean and the Wild Lotus Band was amazing. I started receiving information about what to do with Molly, the mannequin! Spirit suggested I make a short video focusing on what would have happened to the mannequin and bathing suit if the Oklahoma bombing had never happened. I imagined a mother who ends up buying the swimsuit to spend the summer with her kids at the pool. This was a perfect way to honor the fifteen children who died and all the other children whose parents died during the bombing.

When I arrived home, I started experimenting with the few photos I had of the mannequin when it was pulled from the rubble of the Oklahoma City bombing. Then I tried on the bathing suit; surprised that it fit me perfectly. The next day, I got a friend to go with me to the local swimming pool in our neighborhood to shoot some video footage. A few days later, another friend called me. I told her what I was doing; she said she had a great place to film the next scenes. It was an abandoned swimming pool and would be a wonderful contrast to the footage shot at the community pool, providing the perfect setting for a turning point in the film.

Everything fell into place with ease. The entire project was full of magical, synchronistic moments blended together harmoniously. I decided I wanted a spoken word poem for the film's narration and found a local Asheville poet who had visited the Oklahoma City Memorial. I showed him a rough video cut and told him about the remaining storyline.

His hauntingly beautiful spoken word poem blended well with my vision. When he sent me the first draft of the poem, he thought it would need work. Reading it for the first time was a hair-raising, chill-inducing, tear-producing experience. He had captured it perfectly! No changes were needed.

Just a few weeks before going to the recording studio for the project, I attended another kirtan at the West Asheville Yoga Studio. The musicians and singers amazed me that night. I dropped into a trance state. There was something about the tone and voice of the male singer and the way he played the acoustic guitar that spoke to me. As I remained in a trance, I kept hearing the word "freedom."

When I got home, I googled songs with the word "freedom" in them.

The one that caught my eye was the song "*Freedom*" that Richie Havens sang at Woodstock. The minute Richie started singing, I realized the kirtan singer's voice sounded like Richie Havens. Even the way they played their guitars was similar.

I had never realized the Richie Havens "Freedom" song is like kirtan. In many parts of the song, he calls out, and the audience responds. I was in awe of how perfect this song would be to honor those who were injured or killed by the Oklahoma

City bombing. I loved how the song's style was like the kirtan call and response, so I did some extra research about the song.

Richie was the first musician to go onstage at Woodstock. You might recall there were so many people trying to get there that the musicians had difficulty getting to the actual site. The Woodstock producers asked Richie to stretch out his performance time. The song "Freedom" came from an old hymn, "Motherless Child," that Mr. Havens remembered from church. In order to stall until more musicians arrived, Ritchie improvised a fantastic and powerful rendition of this spiritual hymn.

I couldn't think of a better choice—the song talks about freedom, needing our mothers, fathers, brothers, and sisters, and "Sometimes I feel like a motherless child"—all emotions that a tragedy like the Oklahoma City bombing can bring to the surface.

Never would I have expected Spirit to help me so much with an art project. I am still awestruck that Spirit guided me in such detail. Everything continued to fall into place.

I hired a recording producer to record the spoken word poem. He was able to secure a fantastic sax player who had worked with many well-known musicians. The producer accompanied the sax player with the piano, creating the perfect background to the poem.

The musicians and singers I discovered at the West Asheville Yoga kirtan session brought a beautiful mix of guitar and song to the ending credits. I still get chills and tears every time I hear them during the credits of the film.

The project culminated with showings at three different venues in Asheville: Isis Music Hall, The Satellite Gallery, and the Altamont Theatre and Music Hall. The film began with me wearing the bathing suit in the busy community swimming pool to just the mannequin with the suit in the abandoned pool. As the poem builds up a crescendo of emotive language, words hint at the darker and deeper essence of the film. The scenes after the pools mirror the rest of the words in the poem—the Ryder truck, the Federal Building, flowers, signs honoring the victims, the one surviving tree that remained after the bombing, and the 168 bronze chairs representing the people who died, laid out in nine rows, which signified each floor of the Federal Building.

After the film was over, we all held a moment of silence for the lives affected by this tragedy. The Q & A afterward helped people process their emotions. Later, I donated the project to the Oklahoma City National Memorial and Museum.

Synchronicity

It was amazing how Spirit kept directing my attention to so many synchronistic moments and opportunities that allowed an old mannequin with a bathing suit to become a beautiful tribute to the Oklahoma City bombing tragedy. It is all about honoring Divine timing. Slow down and be patient while you open yourself up to receive and honor your Divine guidance.

The more you open yourself and your life to Spirit, the more you receive. All you need to do is ask for help, listen, and remain open. Spirit speaks to us in many ways. It may be through trance states or dreams. Or through what you see or hear in the lyrics in a song, a book, a movie, an encounter with a random stranger or a dear friend, being in nature, listening to sacred music, meditating, or praying. The important thing is to pay attention and not assume everything is random or coincidental.

Chapter 11

2017 – Ecuador: Shaman, Past Lives, Mediumship

———————⟨⟨⟨———————

I almost moved to San Miguel de Allende, Mexico, in my mid-thirties. After my sixtieth birthday, I revisited the idea of leaving the United States and living in a foreign country. After a great deal of research, I narrowed down my choices to Mexico, Ecuador, and Portugal. I made Ecuador my first stop.

When I traveled to Ecuador, my son came with me and stayed for a couple of weeks to help me get settled. My multiple sclerosis was so debilitating; we were not sure if I could endure the trip to Ecuador. My son worried that my cognitive problems would be much worse in a Spanish-speaking country. Although I had studied Spanish in college, he had a difficult time believing I could live in a Spanish-speaking country with my severe memory problems. I promised him I would keep some basic sentences and my address with me at all times.

We encountered a lot of problems with the house I had rented. After the first night, I knew I needed different housing, but I worried about the physical and mental energy required to find another place. My son stepped up and took care of everything. He did all the research and narrowed down places for us to see. We found a great place on the first day of our search. Then he focused on finding out where I could meet expats.

Before he went back to the U.S. he told me, "I am proud of you for having the courage to follow your dreams, despite your illness. Don't worry; if something happens and you cannot stay, I will fly down here and bring you home."

I lived in Ecuador for six months. One of my priorities was finding a shamanic curandero, one who focuses on healing the mind, body, and spirit. They may use herbs, tobacco, reading and clearing a person's energy with an egg, music, songs, prayer, incense, fire ceremonies, essential oils, bodywork, energy healing, plant medicine, shamanic journeying, soul retrieval, spiritual cleansings, and trance work.

The first healing session with Roberto, an Ecuadorian shaman, was a limpia bath to clear and purify my mind, body, and soul. Roberto cooked a big pot of herbs, which he had me pour slowly over my body. It is important to leave the herbs on the body, so you don't dry yourself off. I got dressed and walked into the other room to continue the healing session.

Not only was most of my body and hair still wet, but it was also winter, with no heat in the house. I could not stop shivering. Although Roberto instructed me not to use a towel, he pulled one from his shelf and gently dried my hair. As soon as he touched my head, I started having memories of Roberto and me together in a past life. We were husband and wife Incan healers. I remembered him drying my hair in this way many times in that life.

After drying my hair, he took off his ceremonial hat and placed it on my head. I was very surprised that he put it on my head since it was a sacred hat.

The next day, I spoke with Roberto.

He told me, "I could not stop thinking about you and our session. Since I couldn't sleep, I got up in the middle of the night and went hiking barefoot in the Andes Mountains. I was there most of the night, asking for clarity about healing you."

He suggested a shamanic massage, which combines visualization with manual manipulations and energy work to release stagnant energy and physical, emotional, mental, and spiritual pain. Roberto removed so much negative energy from me during the massage that many times, he had to go in the other room to spit or vomit out the dark energy.

Each time I met with Roberto, I remembered more lifetimes with him. The memories were so vivid they were blurring the lines between the past and the present. Roberto started interacting with me in a more personal way.

He had to leave for a week to go out of town. While there, he texted me several times, mentioning that he missed me. Yes, I know that was not appropriate for a healer to tell a client. But, we were both remembering our deep past life connections, which were confusing us in the present. I missed him too, which had never happened with a healer.

The next time I saw Roberto, we started talking about our memories of our shared past lives.

Roberto told me, "Yes, I had the same memory as you as soon as I touched your head to dry your hair after your herbal limpia bath."

I said, "Since that night, I have had more memories from that life. We lived to old age. People in our tribe loved and respected us. It was a wonderful life."

Roberto nodded and smiled in agreement.

His next revelation stunned me.

"I have had two recurring dreams since childhood. The first one is about ancient Egypt. I am running and hiding in caves and tunnels."

Little Divine tears started rolling down my face—this was the same dream that many of the people I recognized from the ancient Egyptian lifetime told me.

"My other recurring dream is about Paris. I was a server, and there is always the same woman in the dream."

"I am the woman in your Paris dream," I responded.

Never had I met someone where we both remembered having been romantic partners in so many lifetimes! We explored having a relationship with each other in this lifetime. Things ran awry. Roberto, a multigenerational shaman, surprised me when he shared his thoughts.

"You are so far ahead of me spiritually. I don't think I will ever be able to catch up with you. I am also afraid of being the man you knew in our past lives."

As I remembered more details about my relationship with Roberto in the Paris and Egyptian lifetimes, I understood why Roberto pulled away. In Paris, I had many admirers and would not commit to him. I broke his heart.

Later, after doing more past life regressions, I realized I lost my trust in Roberto in Egypt. We both had deep wounds from past lives that seemed to hold us back from being together this lifetime. I doubt if we will try again to be together in this lifetime. Maybe our destiny is to come together in another life or a different dimension.

When I arrived back in the United States, Roberto's Soul Body started appearing. This continued for almost a year. It felt so real—I experienced his Soul Body with all my senses. I became concerned that having his Soul Body around so much would inhibit my ability to have an intimate relationship with someone else in the 3D world. Roberto's Soul Body showed up so often that I feared I was becoming complacent with the situation.

Connections with the departed

Before I left Ecuador, a relative of a friend of mine committed suicide. It was tragic because he left a one-year-old baby and a young wife. My friend told me that the wife was unwilling to accept what happened and convinced herself it was an accident.

One day, I got a nudge from my Spirit Guides that the departed husband wanted to speak to his wife through me to explain what happened. It was heartbreaking to listen to all the details. I silently cried during the session, hearing her deceased husband filled with so much sorrow and regret.

"I don't know if we should tell her everything," I told my friend. "He made it very clear to me he did indeed kill himself. He is very sorry, but it is a lot to handle. Since you're her aunt, you need to be the one who decides what to tell her."

My friend responded, "It's important that she knows the truth; it will help her heal. I understand it will be difficult for her to hear, but I think it's the right thing to do."

When my friend told her niece in Spanish what her husband told me, I felt my heart was going to break.

First, she screamed. Then she started wailing, rocking her body back and forth as if that might shake something loose and allow her to go back to a time before her husband died.

All she could say was, "No! No! No!"

My friend held and comforted her niece, telling her that everything would be okay. I left to give them more privacy.

Chapter 12

Spring 2018: Unexpected Health Crisis

———— ༄༅༄ ————

After returning from Ecuador, I found something bright red, like blood, in my toilet bowl. Assuming something I had eaten was causing it, I decided not to worry. Every few weeks, it would happen again. One day, I also found small pieces of body tissue. I accepted it was vaginal bleeding, not something an older woman should be experiencing.

The next day, my doctor did a Pap smear and ordered a vaginal ultrasound. The day after the ultrasound, I met with the gynecologist. What he said shocked me.

"Based on your symptoms, medical history, and test results, I am concerned you have both uterine and ovarian cancer. I want to schedule several surgical procedures. You will need to agree to let me take out whatever I don't think looks good."

He did not like my response.

"I will agree to surgery, but I need some time to prepare. However, I will not let you take anything out until we have had a detailed conversation and biopsy results after the surgery."

The doctor agreed to give me three weeks and reiterated that he needed me to agree he could remove what he thought was necessary.

I made it a priority to stay calm and centered and not let fear dictate my options. After receiving the doctor's news, I met with a friend to help me put together a healing plan. When I blurted something out, like I was channeling, it surprised both of us.

I said, "The cancer has something to do with Roberto, the Ecuadorian shaman, my son, and my womb."

Since Roberto and my son never met in this lifetime, it made sense that I needed a past life regression. In the past, I had several past life regressions that focused on a past life in ancient Egypt. I already knew Roberto was in that lifetime, so I prepared to revisit it.

During the energetic healing sessions I performed with people I recognized from that Egyptian lifetime, I had pieced together what happened. The Wise Ones' leaders sent a delegation to Egypt to bring the Yin Yang healing. We were all extremely powerful beings. It didn't take long for the Egyptian leaders to demand that we use our power for nefarious purposes.

The Egyptian leaders became agitated each time we refused their demands. We were much more powerful than them; they could never take full control if they didn't get inside help. None of us realized they bribed some Wise Ones to turn on the rest of the group.

They planned an attack to kill all of us. To prevent us from warning the others telepathically, it had to be simultaneous.

Everyone's past life memories about this life are the same. Like the first woman I worked on, they killed many in the temple. A few escaped. They were the ones who had the recurring dreams of being chased, and running and hiding in caves and tunnels in Egypt.

The first time I heard about the dream was in 2010. A group of us sat at my dining room table. One woman told us about a recurring dream she has had since childhood. Another woman began crying at the table.

"Are you okay?" I asked.

"I have experienced that identical dream since I was a child," she responded.

Imagine my surprise when, years later, Roberto, the Ecuadorian shaman, told me he had a recurring dream about Egypt since his childhood. It was a little mind-blowing to hear him describe the dream. Even though he only speaks Spanish and grew up in a completely different environment, he used the same words everyone used to describe what happened in their dreams about Egypt. After hearing this same dream from many people, I started calling them the "runners."

Although I lived in that ancient Egyptian lifetime, I had not yet remembered what happened to me. I realized I wasn't a runner since I did not have any of the dreams of running and hiding in tunnels and caves.

I always trusted I would remember what happened to me in Egypt at the right time. Still, it was a bit nerve-racking to go into this past life regression to deal with the uterine and ovarian cancer. As John began the regression, I prayed for strength to face whatever the session revealed.

The first thing I saw and felt was being stabbed in the belly. I was in the temple, lying down, eyes closed, in deep meditation.

"Oh, my God! I am pregnant. They are killing both me and my baby."

"Who is the father of your baby?" John asked.

Sobbing, I was having difficulty speaking.

"It is Roberto's baby. Why didn't he come back to find us? I need to understand why Roberto ran instead of looking for me."

As John guided me, I observed some members of our group outside working in the fields. In a split second, the Egyptian warriors came running toward them with their swords ready for battle. The Wise Ones started running as fast as they could to enter the caves. Without the ability to transmit and receive telepathic messages, they did not realize others were being murdered.

John's next question challenged me even more.

"Who is stabbing you?"

I took a glance and responded, "I don't recognize who it is."

"Look closer. You need to identify who is murdering you."

"I can't."

"Gaze into their eyes. You know who it is. Don't be afraid. I am here with you."

It made sense that John encouraged me to peer into their eyes. To hold an intentional gaze into someone's eyes is one of the quickest ways to connect with another being's soul energy.

I looked into the eyes of my killer and asked my Spirit Guides to reveal their identity. As soon as they did, my body fell into complete stress overload. With a racing heart, my breathing quickened and became shallow, and my entire body tensed up.

I gasped. Even though this person didn't seem familiar, with the help of my Spirit Guides, I realized I have known them from many other lives.

"Oh, my God. It is my son. He is killing my baby and me. He betrayed us. Why didn't I realize this would happen? It was my responsibility to take care of the group. How could I have not known?"

John's next request overwhelmed me.

"You need to forgive your son and Roberto."

"I can't. This is too much. I am not sure I can move past the betrayal!"

"Chloe, I understand. But the only way to free yourself is to forgive them."

Still struggling with forgiving my son and Roberto, John guided me through a forgiveness process. First, he had me take slow, deep breaths. Then he asked me to repeat after him.

"Roberto, I forgive you for not coming back to rescue us. I now realize you didn't know we were in danger. I forgive you for running away."

After I gave my forgiveness to Roberto, John asked me to take more deep breaths.

"Breathe in the energy of forgiveness. Breathe out your hurt, anger, and disappointment."

We did the same process for my son. John told me to repeat after him.

"I forgive you for betraying the Wise Ones. I forgive you for killing me and my baby in Egypt."

Distraught, I told John, "I'm sorry. I don't think I can forgive him for the murders."

"Chloe, the forgiveness process is for you. Until you can forgive your son, that event will stay stuck in your body and mind. I understand how difficult this is to do. By forgiving him, you are not saying that the murders and other betrayals were okay. It's a way for you to let go of what happened, so we can clear your energy, and you can move on."

As I took a deep breath, I repeated, "I forgive you for betraying the Wise Ones. I forgive you for killing my baby and me in Egypt."

Then, John had me do more deep breathing until I felt no more emotional charge about what my son and Roberto had done in Egypt. John finished our session with a powerful Reiki attunement.

Sound immersion healing

River Guerguerian has always been one of my favorite healers. This healing session was extraordinary. When I first arrived at his studio, he showed me his new drum. The sound was exquisite. It took me to a profoundly sacred place.

Because of my traveling, it had been a while since I had seen River.

"I don't do many sound immersion healings anymore," River shared with me.

"Why? You are such a gifted and amazing sound healer. Why would you stop?"

"I am tired of the people who come to me and aren't willing to do their work. Or, the ones who are afraid to surrender to the process, so they don't receive the full benefit of the experience."

"I understand. I have experienced the same challenge. If a person comes to me for several sessions, and I can tell they have not been doing their work, I will tell them I can't work on them anymore. We are not 'fixers'—alternative healing is a team effort."

"Chloe, I love doing sound immersions with you. You are not afraid to go deep. When you completely surrender, it enhances the experience for me as well."

As always, it was a great sound healing.

For at least thirty minutes after the sound immersion, River seemed to hear my questions before I asked them out loud. Without trying, I was communicating with him telepathically. In my mind, I would think about a question, which he would immediately answer out loud. I had long suspected that River was a Wise One, so it made sense to me I could communicate with him in this way.

River told me he saw cancer in my body.

He explained, "The good news is that right now, it is small. You still have time to get rid of it."

River added, "If there is anything else you need me to do, just let me know."

Shamanic bodywork

I had never met Michael Brasunas, a gentle angelic soul who does sacred shamanic bodywork and energetic healing. Thank goodness I honored my intuition and saw him. His hands became so hot I thought I might have burn marks on my belly. It was like he was incinerating cancer from my body. Then he began making kneading movements on my belly as if to seal the work he had just done. Michael finished everything with long, sweeping movements from the top of my head to the bottoms of my feet to clear any residual cancer or negative energy.

Afterward, he agreed with my perception of what he had done during the session.

Holistic transpersonal session

I love having sessions with Shannon South. It is such a beautiful and powerful spiritual process. I am always amazed how much we can resolve in one hour.

Several healers told me I needed to speak my truth more authentically. It didn't surprise me when this session with Shannon revealed that me getting sick was my body trying to get my attention about honoring my truth, and being willing to share my authentic self. Trust me, when a doctor thinks you may have two types of cancer, you pay attention!

Shannon's process helps you dig deep to uncover the core. Once you find the core issue and talk about it, she invites you to release it by first describing how it looks. Mine looked like sticky black tar. Then she asks you to tell her what it looks like after letting it go from your body. It had transformed the once sticky black tar into a hardened, calcified piece of black lava stone.

I also see images that symbolize the core issue. I saw a yin-yang symbol inside a heart. For me, this represented finding balance and harmony, integrating the masculine and feminine, and a reminder that I have the Yin Yang healing from the Wise Ones' dimension inside of me. I made a pillow with a heart and yin-yang symbol as part of my healing process.

Psychic healer

Bob confirmed what I had already been told—this cancer scare was about me needing to be more authentic. He helped me understand that when I withhold my true thoughts and feelings, it blocks me from being my authentic self. He warned me that if I didn't embrace my true self, I would create an illness in my throat.

His prediction of a potential throat issue caught my attention. I remembered a Reiki session I received in Ecuador from an Italian woman. The entire time she was working on my throat chakra, I thought I was going to throw up. As soon as she moved to a different chakra, the nausea disappeared. After our session, she asked me to think about what I was having difficulty saying. Later, I met with a sound healer from Chile. She also noticed the same issues with my throat chakra and asked me what I was afraid to see and say.

Second sound immersion session

With the surgery date fast approaching, I felt like I needed another session with River. I told him I wanted the entire session with only his new drum. My Spirit Guides suggested instead of lying down that I needed to be standing so that the drum vibration would reach both sides of my body.

I stood in the middle of the room as River walked around me playing the drum. After he began, Divine tears rolled down my cheeks. It transported me to the Wise Ones' dimension. With an overwhelming sense of knowing, I saw that when we were preparing to go into a spiritual battle, we would form a circle. One at a time, we would stand in the middle of the circle while River drummed around us. The vibrations of the drumming would clear and strengthen us.

I noticed a shift in River after this powerful drumming session. He seemed more open to the possibility that he was from the Wise Ones' dimensions.

"Have you ever done any research about the Wise Ones? Has anyone else written about it?"

I responded, "No, I haven't. But that sounds like a good idea. I will let you know what I find."

When I left River, I was still in an altered state. The friend I met for lunch noticed and asked me about my session. When I mentioned the Wise Ones and Egypt, her face turned pale and she started crying.

"What's wrong? Are you okay?" I asked.

In a whisper, she responded, "I never told anyone about my life in Egypt." As she continued to cry, she told me what she remembered.

"I was there. I saw everything. Before anyone could kill me, they scooped me up and took me to another dimension."

It stunned me. "Was anyone else taken?"

She replied, "No. I was the only one. I was pregnant, and they wanted to save the baby."

Now my tears came. "I was also pregnant. The Wise Ones must have grabbed you when they realized the traitors had murdered my baby and me."

Although I had known this woman for over a year, we had never talked much about spiritual matters. What a surprise to find out she was in Egypt and survived the massacre. I understand why she had told no one about this experience. It was so traumatic that most of us had blocked out that lifetime.

Last step: creating a sacred space in the hospital

After three weeks of intensive healing sessions, I knew I needed to continue the spiritual healing work during the hospital stay for the surgical procedures. There are no hard rules about how to create a sacred space. Similar to creating an altar, choose items that serve as visual and energetic reminders of what is important to you spiritually.

The yin yang heart pillow I made was a priority. I kept it on my belly until they rolled me into the operating room. I put crystals from home on my heart, solar plexus, sacral, and root chakras.

My curated list of sacred music brought me comfort and helped me to stay calm and grounded. The music included the channeled Wise Ones' sound immersion session River and I did in 2013, "Journey Through the Chakras" by Ivan Martín Garcia, "Heart of Healing" by Karen Drucker, and "Rhythms of the Chakras" by Glen Velez. I listened to the music during the pre-op, surgery, and while I was in the recovery room.

I also took a beautiful phoenix card with me. When I had run into a friend a few days before the surgery, she channeled this message:

"Chloe, you are going to be fine. You are always the phoenix rising."

The card, a brightly colored drawing in hues of red, orange, yellow, and gold, depicted the Greek mythical bird creature, the phoenix. As the phoenix rises from the fire's ashes in its bird nest, it represents rebirth, transformation, and renewal. The phoenix brings a call to let go of what no longer serves you, to embrace a more enlightened life path. The caption on the card summed up everything I had been working on:

"Choose Transformation and the Passion for Living Will Rise from What You Let Go."

My friend who waited with me until I went into surgery continued to read this message out loud until they rolled me into the operating room.

I have had surgeries in the past; never had I been this calm, peaceful, and grounded. We created such a powerful sacred space that when the hospital staff came in, their demeanor changed. As soon as the surgeon walked into the sacred space, he apologized.

"I am sorry for not listening to you and your wishes. I should have been more compassionate, receptive, and understanding. You offered to have a second surgery if it was necessary. It wasn't right of me to keep insisting that you had to permit me to remove anything today. I hope you can accept my apology."

Then, right before I was going into surgery, the anesthesiologist returned. She reversed her initial decision to give me traditional anesthesia since I experience a great deal of nausea and vomiting with it. Rather than trying to counter it with anti-nausea medicine, she switched to a different anesthesia. She gave me an injection, and then they started rolling my gurney. The last thing I remember was seeing a glimpse of the Soul Body of Roberto, the Ecuadorian shaman, as he passed silently through the halls.

Good news

My follow-up appointment was a few days later. It surprised the doctor that everything looked good during the surgery. However, as a precaution, he did a cancer rinse to check if cancer cells were in the peritoneal cavity. The biopsies and cells from the cancer rinse were negative.

Happy with all the healing work I did before the surgery, it wasn't surprising to me that the doctor gave me good news. The entire three weeks I had all the alternative healing work done, I focused on the lessons coming up during the healings rather than going down a path full of fear of having cancer. Except for the initial shock of hearing my doctor tell me he thought I had two kinds of cancer, I had very few moments thinking about whether I had cancer, and how that might affect my life.

Chapter 13

2018: San Miguel de Allende, Mexico
Healings, Activations, & Initiations

─────────── ༄ ༄ ༄ ───────────

I lived in a Mexican neighborhood just a short walk from Centro, in an amazing two-story house in an artist compound. Bennie was the first person I met at the compound. We connected on many levels. In a brief period of time, our conversation turned to spirituality.

She started telling me about a friend who told her years ago about a lifetime Bennie had in Egypt. It stunned me. I had only been in San Miguel for a few days, still unpacking and getting settled. Having not given much thought about whether I would meet anyone there from the ancient Egyptian lifetime, here was Bennie sitting beside me, bringing it up.

"What did your friend tell you about that lifetime?" I asked.

"She said something terrible happened, and she helped me escape. A large rock hid an entrance to a tunnel. She moved the rock and told me to run as fast as possible. My friend said there would be more tunnels and caves and that I should always stay hidden."

When I meet people from the Egyptian lifetime, I always let them talk before saying anything.

"What else did your friend tell you about that lifetime?" I asked.

Bennie answered, "She wouldn't tell me anything else. She said it was horrible."

I took a deep breath and said, "Your friend is right. It was terrible. Are you ready to find out what happened?"

Bennie turned and looked at me, bewildered, and asked, "How do you know what happened?"

"I started remembering that lifetime ten years ago. I have met many people from that life and was able to piece together what happened."

As I told Bennie what transpired, she sat motionlessly. Then little tears rolled down her cheeks. Everyone in that ancient Egyptian lifetime experienced the same shock, anguish, and grief when we started talking about what happened.

Noticing how people react to the information became one of my ways to confirm they were from that lifetime. A genocide this horrific would bring tears to anyone's eyes who witnessed and experienced it.

Once the floodgates opened for Bennie, she started remembering more. Together, we achieved greater clarity about that lifetime.

My connection with Bennie continued to amaze me. The first time she and her partner did a shamanic drumming journey with me, I recognized her energy was the same as the Native American chief who had shown up as a Spirit Guide for the first few in-person energy healings I did.

Shamanic drumming journeys are used to enter a trance state and visit other dimensions. A drum played with a tempo of four beats per second can induce an altered state. Other methods of shamanic journeying might include song, dance, chanting, meditating, or shaking a rattle or other percussion instruments.

The second time they did a shamanic drumming journey at my house, I dropped into a deep trance. That night, the drumming sounded almost identical to my healer friend River Guerguerian's drumming. The sound was so similar, as if River was in the room playing. Since I was in a deep trance with my eyes closed, I didn't recognize who was channeling River's drumming. As soon as they finished, I opened my eyes.

As I pointed to the middle of the room, I asked, "Who drummed in that space?"

"I did," Bennie responded. "Why are you asking?"

"Your drumming tonight is identical to my healer and friend River Guerguerian. You are his drumming doppelgänger."

Before she left, I suggested she might want to look at River's website.

"I think you might remember River from other lifetimes."

I received a succinct message from Bennie.

"Yes, I know him."

My next encounter with someone in San Miguel from the Egyptian lifetime was with another neighbor. I don't recall how or why we started talking about Egypt. Like many people I met from ancient Egypt, Tom started sobbing when we talked about the Wise Ones being murdered. However, unlike my other encounters, I didn't see his role in Egypt. I think I was so taken by how much grief he had that I assumed over time it would become clear what role he played. Two years later, I wondered if Tom had been a Wise One traitor.

A local Mexican healer's husband, Fred, asked me to do an energy healing. I explained that my ability to tap into other people's past lives depends on my Spirit Guides and the person's willingness to surrender to the process. I wasn't expecting Fred to be connected to the ancient Egyptian lifetime. Yet, toward the end of the session, I saw him running as he headed for the caves. An Egyptian, brandishing a sword up in the air while he rode his horse, aimed for Fred. In one quick fell swoop, the sword pierced Fred's back, extending out from his stomach.

Later, a young person moved into the artist compound. We started talking about spirituality. It shocked me when she mentioned the Wise Ones.

"You know about the Wise Ones?" I asked.

"Yes, I have known about them for a while," she answered.

"Does ancient Egypt mean anything to you?" I asked her.

"No, why?" she asked.

"I have been remembering and meeting people from a past life in Egypt for the past ten years. It involves the Wise Ones. I never met anyone who knew about the Wise Ones who didn't also have a connection to the ancient Egyptian lifetime. I thought maybe I made up the name."

"Oh no, you didn't make it up," she assured me.

Charco del Ingenio – botanical garden

It amazed me when I realized the deep connection these desert gardens in San Miguel have with the ancient Egyptian lifetime. One morning, I woke up with an overwhelming urge to go to the Charco botanical gardens. As soon as I arrived, I became altered. Everything was so familiar. I wasn't sure if I was remembering things from the past, or if I was in the past, visiting the future.

Upon my first glimpse of the pool that sits between the deep cavernous walls of the gorge, I started having visions of some of my fellow Wise Ones from the Egyptian lifetime. I could see that we lived here in El Charco many lifetimes ago. When I looked directly at the pool area, I saw everything. I recognized Roberto, Bennie, and River. Roberto and I were shamanic healers, and Bennie and River were our tribe's drummers.

It was like watching a movie. Even more strange, I only had the visions if I looked directly at the pool. It was as if a vortex opened when I held my gaze on the pool.

Bennie came with me the next time I visited the gardens. Once again, my visions about our lifetime there were crystal clear. As long as I looked at the pool, I could see everything. I began wondering if the Wise Ones wanted us to perform some type of ceremony at El Charco.

Since I began channeling information from the Wise Ones' dimension in 2008, I have been given information on a "need-to-know" basis. Therefore, I don't move forward with any spiritual work involving the Wise Ones unless I am clear that I am being guided to do so by them. Although my visions were very strong each time I visited El Charco, I never received final guidance from them about having a Wise Ones ceremony at the gardens.

When I got back to the United States, I had another session with Michael, the shamanic healer and bodyworker. In the past, Michael had shared with me he had not had a past life recollection, which made this session even more amazing. About halfway through the bodywork, he stopped to ask me a question.

"Chloe, I am receiving some important information about your life in Egypt. Is it okay if I stop what I am doing to tell you about it?"

"Of course," I answered.

He continued, "You are being asked to forgive what happened in Egypt."

I responded, "I already did that in my last past life regression. It was difficult, but with the help of the regression therapist, I forgave Roberto and my son."

"No, now you are being asked to forgive everyone—the perpetrators and the victims. You also need to forgive yourself. I understand you blame yourself, that somehow you should have known and been able to stop it."

Overwhelmed with grief, at first, I wasn't able to respond.

"No one saw it coming—not even the leaders of the Wise Ones' dimension. I think that is why the Wise Ones didn't want us to have a ceremony in San Miguel. Until they are certain of why and how this happened in Egypt, they don't want us to do anything that might rekindle our powers."

Sacred shamanic encounters

I resonate with shamanic work. Sometimes, it is difficult to find an authentic shaman curandero, a respected healer and spiritual leader in the community. When I lived in Ecuador, it took me a month to find one. It is much easier to find a shaman if all you want is a hallucinogenic plant medicine experience like ayahuasca.

During my time in San Miguel de Allende, I met with Q'eros Andean Pagos Don Humberto Sonco. The Peruvian Q'eros are the direct descendants of the Incas. Because they are so dedicated to preserving their indigenous customs, no outsiders were allowed to visit until 1996. Pagos are the spiritual leaders and healers of the Q'eros Nation.

I had a Karpay Initiation and Activation by Pagos Don Humberto. This ceremony opens up the chakras to connect to the Andean energy and wisdom to understand and access abilities that have been unused because of blockages. I experienced a significant shift of increased peace, happiness, wisdom, clarity, awareness, and heightened senses.

Later I found Eduardo Morales, an amazing shamanic curandero who lives in Tepoztlán. He and his wife came to San Miguel de Allende once a month to offer their healing services. My first session with Eduardo focused on my relationship with my son. I returned for two more sessions to complete the work relating to my son.

Most of the time, Eduardo gives you homework, which I love. For the healing work with my son, he instructed me to find a safe place to burn candles, so they could burn all the time. I put the candles on my tiled fireplace mantle, along with a photo of my son. Each time I lit a candle, I said a blessing, intending to heal and strengthen my relationship with my son.

I dedicated my next three sessions with Eduardo to removing Roberto from my energy field. Roberto's Soul Body had been visiting me for almost a year. It felt like it was becoming unhealthy in the third dimension world to allow this to continue. I had tried many remedies, and nothing had stopped him from showing up.

"I think Roberto attached himself to my energy field," I told Eduardo.

After Eduardo began the session, he shared what he had seen with me.

"You are right. He attached his energetic field to yours. Don't worry; I can remove him."

After three sessions, Roberto no longer appeared in my mind or energy field. Considering I had tried so many things to remove Roberto, I was very impressed that Eduardo had succeeded. It was a relief not to have Roberto's Soul Body around all the time.

During my last month in San Miguel, I had another appointment with Eduardo. This time, I was ready for a huge miracle.

"I am so grateful for the fantastic results with your work on me. So, this next request is huge. I want you to remove my multiple sclerosis."

Eduardo responded, "Okay. Let's get you on the table so I can check in with your soul and Spirit Guides and see what they say."

This "check-in" period was much longer than my other sessions with Eduardo. That made sense since this would be a much bigger healing challenge.

"The good news is that yes, I can do it. Would you be able to have five more sessions this week? The guides said it will take six sessions."

"Of course! Just tell me when, and I will be here," I exclaimed.

Eduardo instructed me to avoid all alcohol and other substances for the next two weeks. This healing was extremely important to me, so I also remained in a meditative state during that time.

I completed six sessions with Eduardo that week. For the last session, he asked me to bring a flower and a jar. The entire time I lived in San Miguel, I surrounded myself with sunflowers. When asked to bring flowers to my Karpay Initiation and Activation, I chose sunflowers. So, I brought a sunflower for this final healing session with Eduardo. He filled the jar with rainwater and told me that at the end of the session, he would use the sunflower to sprinkle the water all over my body. Afterward, he put the sunflower in the jar and gave it to me.

"You must keep the jar in sunlight every day for a month. On the thirtieth day, I want you to bury the remains of the sunflower. Once you complete the burial ceremony, don't look back."

I chose a remote spot in the yard so that I would not look back at it. As I am writing this, I realize "not looking back" also referred to the multiple sclerosis. It was time to let go of the past and move forward in a new and healthy way.

My life changed drastically, in a good way. I felt normal again. It was like my body was reborn. This was one of the biggest healing miracles I have ever experienced.

Chapter 14

Europe Awakens More Past Life Memories

Europe was the last stop on my quest to find the next place where I wanted to live. I planned to stay in Porto for six weeks. During that time, I also visited several other cities in Portugal, all charming. I left Porto early since it didn't seem Portugal would be my choice.

As soon as I got off the metro in Athens, Greece, I felt at home. I loved the vibrancy and the passion. I realized that is what I missed in Portugal.

I looked forward to visiting the Temple of Zeus. As soon as I entered the grounds, little Divine tears started rolling down my cheeks. One part of the ruins mesmerized me. I couldn't move or take my eyes off of it. A memory of the past life regression I experienced in 2008 appeared. They ambushed and murdered us as my husband, baby, and I stood on the steps of a temple in Greece.

I wrote to my son about the past life memories and my emotional experience at the Zeus temple since he was my son in that past life. Expecting he would say it was just a coincidence or my imagination, his response took me by surprise.

"Well, that makes sense. Don't you remember, my favorite book as a child was about Greek mythology? And in college, I found my Greek mythology class captivating."

I forgot about his mythology book.

When I took a Greek mythology course in college, I experienced the same thing. I loved it so much I considered changing my major.

The next day I went to the Acropolis. It was stunning to be standing amid all that history. Expecting that I would have a similar reaction, it surprised me to have no memories or powerful emotions about the Acropolis.

After several days in Athens, I flew to Crete. As the taxi driver drove me to my rental, he pointed out an island in the shape of a crocodile.

"Legend says that Zeus was born on that island. They made it look like a crocodile to protect him."

My decision to go to Athens and Crete had been a spontaneous last-minute decision. After my powerful reaction at the Zeus temple and later hearing the legend of Zeus being born on that island off Crete, I realized Spirit had directed me to come here. No coincidence that I had a perfect view of Zeus's crocodile island from my apartment.

My trip to the Palace of Knossos was even more revealing. The largest of all the ancient Minoan palaces in Crete, Homer mentions it in his epic "Odyssey" poem. Plato's dialogues about the mythical Atlantis also refer to Knossos. I was most drawn to see the Palace of Knossos because many women held powerful positions as goddesses in ancient Minoan culture.

Known to be one of the most famous archeological sites in the world, the Knossos palace was the center of political, social, and cultural activities of the Minoan civilization during the Bronze Age. The palace built a sophisticated system for water and lighting.

After visiting the Palace of Knossos, I took a second trip into town to the Heraklion Archaeological Museum. There were many statues, drawings, paintings, and pottery depicting women adorned with snakes. It took my breath away as I thought about how many snakes have been in my life.

When the snakes first started appearing in my current life, I knew the snake was one of my spirit animals. But I resisted accepting it. During my visit to the museum, I experienced déjà vu when I realized I had been a goddess at the palace. It also stunned me to witness the similarities in this exhibit to ancient Egypt. There is a strong connection between the two civilizations, and I was a part of both of them.

As soon as I left the museum, I experienced a powerful urge to find a snake bracelet. I knew it was time to embrace and honor the snake as one of my power animals.

I assumed I had completed my spiritual journey in Greece and Crete. A few nights before I left, I booked a trip to a restaurant in the mountains of Crete. As the bus wove through winding mountainous roads, I had another moment of déjà vu. I recognized everything from a lucid dream I had several years before this trip. In the dream, it seemed very familiar, like I had lived there in another life. Now I realize why I saw snakes everywhere in that dream.

The other past life place I visited was Paris. Since I received messages about being a cancan dancer in Paris, I was excited about going to Montmartre and the Moulin Rouge. Even though the original building burned down in 1915, they rebuilt it in 1921. I wept as I stood in front of it. Images started coming to me of Roberto, the Ecuadorian shaman. He worked at the Moulin Rouge as a server in that Paris lifetime. I had been a favorite dancer with many wealthy admirers. Roberto wanted to make a life with me. Quite wild and indulgent in that lifetime, I could never commit to him, which broke his heart.

During my time there, I couldn't get enough of Paris. Everything seemed familiar. I would walk through the neighborhoods for hours, soaking up the Parisian energy and past life memories. I loved Paris so much that I considered putting it on my possible list for places to live. At the very least, I would like to go again for a much longer stay.

When my son was growing up, I used to tell him about the funny sound the ambulances make in Paris. Since he knew I had never visited there this lifetime, he would always tease me about my ambulance sound memories. When he called on my birthday, I was standing on a bridge overlooking the Seine River, close to the Left Bank. An ambulance drove by as we were talking. My son laughed as he heard the ambulance—the sound was the same as I had described to him all these years.

Chapter 15

Making Peace with Visions that Predicted Worldwide Disaster

I traveled for a couple of years to see where I wanted to live next. Besides Portugal, France, Greece, and Crete, I also visited Italy and Spain during my 2019 trip to Europe. Thinking I might choose Portugal, a conversation I had with some expats I met in Porto surprised me.

"Are you excited about moving to Portugal?"

"No. I am still trying to decide where I want to live."

"What other countries are you considering?"

"The two major contenders besides Portugal are Mexico and Ecuador."

"Do you have stronger feelings for any of them?"

"Yes, I can't seem to get Mexico out of my head. I love everything about it—the culture, the Indigenous population, the food, the land, the art. I grew up in Texas, with frequent trips to

Mexico. When I lived in San Miguel de Allende in 2018, I felt blessed to be there every single day."

"Wow! Your whole body lights up when you talk about Mexico. You are glowing, you have a huge smile on your face, and you have a twinkle in your eyes. None of that was happening when you talked about any of the other countries. Based on your body's reaction, I would say Mexico is a good choice for you."

I kept an open mind throughout my European trip. But my heart kept comparing every place to San Miguel de Allende, Mexico. Finally comfortable choosing where I wanted to live, it caught me off-guard to find out three days before I left Europe, that San Miguel's crime rate had drastically increased since I lived there in 2018.

Not sure what to do, I discussed it with some expat friends over lunch. I was living in Aguda Beach, a small fishing village, a short train ride to Porto, Portugal. We went to my favorite restaurant with tables right on the beach where you can see and hear the waves crashing in the ocean. My kind of heaven—bright sun, a light cool breeze, the smell of salt water, and being barefoot in the sand. Aguda Beach will be at the top of my list if I ever live in Portugal.

My friend's succinct advice was exactly what I needed to hear.

"You will have about six months before you want to move from the United States. A lot might happen in San Miguel during that time."

I responded, "That's true. But how can I go back and start selling everything if I am uncertain where I will move?"

"Chloe, you have already decided to leave the United States. I suggest you trust the process. Go back home and get rid of your possessions. Take a leap of faith that either San Miguel's crime rate will go down, or you will find another place where you want to live."

"Besides, it is not like you need to find a forever place before you can let go of the United States. You already made the big decision that you want to live the life of an expat. Just pick a place that will be the starting point for you. The beauty of being an expat is that the entire world is your home—you can live anywhere."

I took my friend's advice to heart, and came home and sold most of my possessions. San Miguel was still struggling with a high level of crime, so I waited until a month before leaving the U.S. to choose Oaxaca City as my first stop. When I arrived in Mexico, I didn't rush to explore Oaxaca. I enjoyed experiencing it by just relaxing and staying in the moment.

I took a trip to the Oaxaca beaches in early March. A few days after my arrival, I started receiving texts from friends that COVID-19 was causing serious havoc in multiple countries. Each day, the texts became more frequent and alarming. I did some online research. Shocked how much had changed in the world in a matter of days, I realized Mexico would be next.

I cut my trip short to return to Oaxaca City to prepare for an inevitable lockdown. On my last day at Zipolite Beach, Canada announced that all Canadians needed to return to their country. The entire day, people frantically checked the news on their cell phones while trying to decide what to do. The strong current of impending doom permeated the air as a contrast to the beauty and warmth of the relaxing beach and inviting ocean.

We all put on a brave face, but a sense of uncertainty surrounded us. Oblivious to how an extended lockdown would affect our lives, we knew to soak up all the sun, sand, and water that day. When it was time to leave, one woman leaned over and gave me a sweet kiss on the cheek. Little did I realize it would be my last kiss for two years.

Like most people, I stocked up on supplies when I got home. Much of the world was in lockdown. A huge layer of guilt engulfed me. I had been having visions of a worldwide disaster since 2010.

When I first started having the visions, I experienced an underlying sense of responsibility for either preventing the disaster or being prepared for what to do if it happened. I organized a group of people, including many healers. We were unaware of when it would happen, but we all realized things were shifting and would eventually create major chaos.

In 2010, I bought a cabin on 7.5 acres in the Smoky Mountains of North Carolina. The property had many natural springs, and wild blackberries grew everywhere. There was room to house lots of people and plenty of land for planting food to eat. It would be a safe house if things in the world started falling apart. In the meantime, I fixed it up to make it more liveable.

If a colossal disaster happened, the plan was for our group to move to the cabin. Everyone had unique skills to offer, which would help us sustain the property and ourselves.

After seven years of no worldwide disaster, and my desire to leave the United States, I sold the cabin. I didn't make this decision lightly. It took me almost two years to be certain that I should let it go.

Having fallen in love with the property, it took another year after I sold it to accept that it was no longer my path. Some of my most peaceful times were at the cabin. I learned how to can food and built a root cellar to store it. My property went to the top of the mountain; it was glorious to hike. I created lots of wonderful memories at this magical property.

It also had a potent spiritual quality to it. When I was there, I could feel spirits. During the remodeling of the cabin, my contractor sent me photos of the daily progress. What caught my immediate attention were the orbs captured in the photos. Orbs can look like a ball of light in photos. I believe orbs are Divine energy, most likely Spirit Guides, angels, or loved ones who have passed. I found it interesting that the orbs only showed up in the photos of certain areas of the cabin.

One day, my contractor sent me photos of the work they had done in the cabin's living room. The photos were full of so many orbs! A few days later, I received a call from the real estate agent who sold the cabin.

She asked, "Is anyone staying in the cabin right now?"

I answered, "No. It is still being remodeled. Why are you asking?"

"We just drove by there, and smoke was coming out of the chimney. If no one is there, I am afraid there is a fire. My husband and I will call the fire department."

Later, the agent called me with more details.

"When the first fire truck arrived, they did not want to force the door open. A log cabin is like a tinderbox, and we knew how quickly this fire could get out of control. So, my husband took responsibility for breaking the door to open it. Three other fire trucks arrived. They put the fire out and are now assessing what might have caused it."

I consider it a miracle that the real estate agent "happened" to be driving on that country road at exactly that time and noticed the smoke coming from the chimney. If she had not seen it and called the fire department when she did, the cabin would have probably burned to the ground.

That evening I pulled out the recent photos from the cabin living room. Stunned, I realized that the number of orbs in the photos had multiplied in the area where the fire was burning. The next day I asked two people from our group to look at the photos. I told them about the fire but did not mention the orbs. When I showed them the photos with the orbs, they sat staring at them.

One woman broke the silence.

"Is anyone else seeing the number of orbs increasing in these photos?"

I exclaimed, "Yes! I didn't want to say anything until you both saw the photos. They are literally multiplying right now before our eyes!"

Since some orbs were already in the photos before the fire, we concluded they were the ones that made sure the real estate agent saw the fire and called for help. We decided the orbs continued to multiply to bring extra protection to the cabin.

Another interesting spiritual occurrence at the cabin was during a terrible snowstorm that lasted for days. The roads were all closed; I couldn't leave the cabin because of the snow. I got up one morning and saw foot tracks in the snow near the cabin. What was significant about the tracks was that they started and ended in the middle of the yard. How could a person have landed and left in the middle of the yard, with no tracks showing where they came from or where they went?

I kept the cabin for seven years. It still brings a smile to my face when I think about my experiences there.

Asking Spirit about the visions of the future

I didn't understand why I was given all these visions if I could not prevent the worldwide disaster and tragedies. They were heartbreaking—so much upheaval, tragedy, and suffering.

I asked my Spirit Guides, "Why can't you prevent this from happening? Why do so many people have to suffer?"

"We are waiting until more people wake up. On your planet, everyone has free will. Those who want a different life will have to make that choice. We can't make that decision for them."

I responded, "So, you will not stop it from happening?"

"No. But we will come afterward to help heal and rebuild."

My heart sank.

Spirit gave me those visions ten years before the pandemic. I am still trying to get clarity. My visions always showed me gathering healers to help heal and rebuild in the aftermath. None of the visions showed me stopping the disaster.

Still, when it became clear that COVID-19 would be a long-term problem, it racked me with guilt. My mind swirled with questions and regrets.

I tried to make more sense of what was happening. I had ten years to stop it. Now it was here. Is this somehow my fault since I knew ten years ago that something like this would happen? Even though my Spirit Guides told me they would not stop it, I felt guilty that I had all this forewarning but did not prevent it from happening.

I agree with my Spirit Guides; this disaster is a huge wake-up call. Still, I couldn't shake the guilt about knowing it was coming and not being able to stop it. My mind and heart were spinning. I felt sad, confused, and upset.

Since I didn't prevent it, I wondered if I could do anything now that the pandemic was here? First, I gathered healers via Zoom. After the first session, Spirit told me this was not the direction I needed to take. So, I intensified my spiritual practice and waited for my Spirit Guides to direct me. In the meantime, I increased my meditation, prayers, listening to sacred music, and staying more grounded and present.

In April 2020, I had a remote session with a local shaman in Oaxaca. She told me that although she and her shamanic colleagues had not seen earlier visions like me, they all knew there was much more going on than just the pandemic. She encouraged me to accept that it was too late to do anything; she said everything was already in motion. It would not be the first time our world failed, nor would it be the last.

Still struggling, I had another session with her in May 2020. I saw thousands of people who had died from COVID-19 confused, unable to leave the earthly realm. Sobbing, I told the shaman we needed to help these souls go to the light. I led a spontaneous ceremony to release them.

The pandemic has been a big lesson in patience for me. Waiting for directions from my Spirit Guides, surviving extreme lockdown in a new city and country where I knew very few people, and being gentle with myself as I searched for answers. It was a challenge.

Chapter 16

Dark Night of the Soul

———— ⌒✺⌒ ————

I remained in strict lockdown in Oaxaca City for seventy-five days. My landlady and her family checked on me frequently and even bought me flowers and a gift on my birthday, which fell on Mother's Day. Several of the organic stores, farms, and restaurants offered deliveries. I also found someone who would shop and run miscellaneous errands for me. The only time I left my small apartment was to meet the delivery people or spend time on the rooftop terrace.

The isolation became overwhelming. It was hot in Oaxaca, which affected how much time I spent on the rooftop. I had rented a small apartment before Covid 19 arrived in Mexico; it didn't seem that important because I thought I would be out most of the time exploring the area. After a while, being confined to a small apartment during extreme lockdown felt suffocating. There were only three rooms—the bedroom, bathroom, and open living, dining, and kitchen area.

I was still grappling with confusion about why Spirit gave me all the visions ten years before the pandemic. It brought up memories I had been experiencing for twelve years, about the ancient Egyptian lifetime. They had sent my group from the Wise Ones' dimension to Egypt to heal the world with the powerful Yin Yang healing. We failed that time; a few traitors from our group helped the Egyptians kill almost all of us.

I wondered if I was being given another opportunity to save the world. Why had I remembered so much from that ancient Egyptian lifetime? Why had I met so many people who were in Egypt with me? Were my visions about an upcoming worldwide disaster connected to my experience in ancient Egypt?

I could not shake the feeling that Spirit wanted me to help heal the world.

In that ancient Egyptian lifetime, all of us knew how to do the Yin Yang healing. I believe that ability is still there, but none of us remember how to do it. Egypt was such a traumatic experience; I think we all blocked it from our memory.

When I first started having the ancient Egyptian memories, I made a conscious decision not to remember how to do the Yin Yang healing. Although curious and intrigued, I never wanted to have another experience like we had in Egypt. I trust if the Wise Ones want me to use it, they will communicate with me. Since the Yin Yang healing is the most powerful healing that exists, and a big reason we were all killed, I hope they will just direct my body on what to do if they ever want me to use it again.

While I was living in Ecuador, a healer and I traded healing sessions. She did not remember a lifetime in Egypt but had memories of living on other planets where I had lived. In our prior discussions, I mentioned the Wise Ones and the Yin Yang healing because I thought I could trust her. When I was performing her healing, she kept telling me to ask the Wise Ones how to do the Yin Yang healing.

I told her, "The Wise Ones will reveal the details of the Yin Yang healing when it is time. It is their decision, not mine."

She persisted with her desire to learn how to do the Yin Yang healing, at one point bypassing me and asking the Wise Ones herself. They ignored her questions, and I ended our session.

To me, it was a huge red flag for her to be so pushy about trying to learn how to do the Yin Yang healing. She was not in ancient Egypt, nor was she from the Wise Ones' dimension. I am protective and respectful of the Wise Ones. If the Yin Yang healing got into the wrong hands, it could be catastrophic. The Egyptians murdered us because of our knowledge and abilities. Neither I nor the Wise Ones' leaders ever want what happened in Egypt to be repeated.

After seventy-five days spent in extreme lockdown, I accepted Covid would not blow over soon. I was deep into an extended dark night of the soul, a time when a person goes through hard lessons and transition.

Before leaving the United States, I had called Bob, my psychic healer. My vet told me it was time to put my dog down, and I wanted him to check in to see if there were any other options.

"I am sorry, Chloe. It is time. Your dog is telling me he is miserable, confused, and scared all the time. I understand how difficult this is, but it would be cruel to let your dog continue to struggle."

Happy to have clarity about my dog, it stunned me when Bob revealed the next thing his guides wanted me to know.

"So, Chloe, what are you up to these days?"

"I am moving to Mexico."

He became silent. Then he said he had something important to tell me.

"I don't want to alarm you, but the guides are telling me you are going to have an exit point show up soon."

"What is an exit point?" I asked.

"It's a time you might leave this world."

"Would I be permanently leaving? Are you talking about death?"

"Yes, death. But it is not definite. There are always circumstances that could change the outcome. For now, they want you to be aware it is a possibility. This is not the time to take risks or do anything reckless."

Now I wondered, is the exit Bob mentioned connected to Covid-19? If so, is it best for me to remain in Mexico or go back to the United States? I needed to have another session with Bob.

He said, "Well, this is interesting. The guides say that the exit point will no longer happen now. They recommend you stay in Mexico."

I asked, "Is that common for an exit to change course before it happens?"

Bob answered, "I am not sure how frequently that happens. But I am getting a clear message you need to stay in Mexico."

Because of my challenges with isolation in my small apartment, Bob suggested I find a larger place to live during the pandemic. He also recommended I consider getting another dog.

I had not planned to get a dog so soon; my dog had only passed six months ago. About three days after my session with Bob, a precious mini French poodle picture popped up on Facebook. It was destiny—Zooey became a part of my family, replacing my sense of isolation with her loving, constant companionship.

Like my other dog, Zooey is a soul companion. She can see spirits. I am aware of their energy and communicate telepathically with them. Zooey and I make an excellent team for spirits stuck in limbo or who want to give a message to loved ones who are still here on earth. She is usually the first to alert me to let me know a spirit needs help.

Because of the heat in Oaxaca, I looked for a place in another city. I narrowed my choices down to San Cristobal de las Casas, Chiapas, or Patzcuaro, Michoacán. Both are mountain towns in Mexico. While talking with Eduardo, who has lived in Mexico his whole life, he suggested I would be happier in Patzcuaro. Since I had never been there, or San Cristobal, I took his suggestion. In less than two weeks, I found a place to live in Patzcuaro, hired a driver, and we made the eleven-hour drive to my new home.

Eduardo was right; Patzcuaro is a good fit for me. It is a charming, authentic, small Mexican mountain town. I can walk almost anywhere, and there is plenty of nature. Content to have a good place to ride out the pandemic, it surprised me how many spiritual things started opening up for me once I began living in Patzcuaro. Spirit had created circumstances that would make me want to leave Oaxaca and live in Patzcuaro. Just when I thought my life would settle into a normal routine in Patzcuaro, I started having new visions and messages from Spirit.

Chapter 17

Fall 2020: Major Spiritual and Personal Transformations

***

Patzcuaro, a five-hundred-year-old small mountain town in Central Mexico, is one of Mexico's Pueblo Magico destinations. Pueblo Magico cities have preserved the original architecture, history, traditions, and culture of their area. With its cobblestone streets, this charming town has temperate weather all year round and an abundance of nature to enjoy. The name Patzcuaro means "Gate of Heaven." Besides the heavenly sense of living in the clouds at a 7,200-foot elevation, they also believed the gods ascended and descended here.

My upstairs neighbor, realizing how difficult it was to move across Mexico to a new place in the middle of a pandemic, reached out to me. She showed me around my new city and introduced me to her friends. We walked everywhere. I loved finding out the best produce stands, restaurants with outdoor dining, hiking trails, stores, and markets.

As a thank you, I invited her to a meal outside in the courtyard. I made octopus soup. The next day, I woke up sick, like I had food poisoning. It surprised me that my neighbor was fine.

I was sick for twenty-four hours. Then it disappeared. Afterward, I had a shamanic session with Eduardo to find out more about why I got sick.

"Chloe, tell me what you put in the soup."

"Just octopus, broth, and some vegetables."

"And your neighbor, who ate the same food as you, did not get sick?"

"No. Is that weird?"

"Sometimes, not everyone will get sick from the same food. The guides are telling me the octopus made you sick to get your attention. The octopus and the water spirits are working with you to enhance and deepen your spiritual abilities. It is an honor to be supported by them."

So many unusual things have happened in my life; I have learned to remain open and go with the flow. Eduardo and I have a deep connection. I trust him and his guides. Spirit gets your attention with whatever means is best. For me, many times, that means affecting me physically.

Water spirits have strong supernatural powers. They love to help with healing, dreamwork, intuition, increasing psychic awareness and abilities, and transformation.

Eduardo continued, "You are beginning a huge transformation. Everything in your life is going to change; nothing will be the same."

I responded, "What interesting timing! I've been contemplating writing a book about my healing and awakening spiritual journey. However, I am a little nervous about revealing everything. Since my life has been so far out, part of me wants to shield myself by writing the book as fiction. I am unsure if I am ready to reveal all that has happened to me on my journey as a true story. It is one thing to talk to you—very different to share it publicly for so many people to see and read."

"Chloe, it is time to share your truth with the world. I understand your concern about telling it in such a big way. Your story is powerful. Let go of any fear. People need to hear it. There is no coincidence that you are writing this book just as this new transformation is beginning. Trust that you are being supported and protected by the spirit world."

The fact the water spirits are guiding and protecting me warms my heart and soul. I realized when Eduardo told me what an honor it is to have the water spirits help; it assured me I would not be writing this book alone. Worries and concerns dropping from my body and mind brought a newfound sense of peace.

Honoring the water spirits

When something extraordinary happens, I like to mark it with a visual reminder. I found a street vendor in Patzcuaro selling beautiful wooden primitive sculptures. The mermaid and merman were the perfect way to mark my encounters with the water spirits. Since I love angels so much, I also bought a flying angel sculpture and a few other angel sculptures. This constant visual reminder that the water spirits are helping me is comforting.

I began embracing the idea of writing my book as a memoir. After all, the world needs plenty of help right now. Climate change disasters, a worldwide pandemic, racism, cruelty to others, intolerance, interfering with people's rights, major social unrest, and political structures teetering on the brink of collapse; I realized I was facing an "If not now, then when" moment. It was time for me to face my fear and move forward with telling the world what I know.

The words started flowing out of me with ease, which I took as confirmation that I was on the right track. Whenever worries crop up about what people will think of me after reading this book, I remind myself that I am on a spiritual mission. My immediate goal is to trust Spirit and continue writing the book. This is about me honoring my guidance and my journey.

Spirit is always offering us lessons. If we ignore the lessons, they keep returning. It is much easier to look at the lessons and deal with them instead of pretending they don't exist. Sometimes, if I am uncertain what a lesson is trying to teach me, I will sit with it until I have more clarity. Leaning into the feelings that are coming up around the lesson is helpful.

"Have I experienced these feelings before?"

"What am I afraid to see or say?"

"What do you want me to notice?"

"How is this connected to my past?"

"What do you want me to do?"

Sometimes you receive answers quickly. Other times, Spirit may reveal to you over time what the essence of a particular lesson is for you. Or you might get someone to assist you in processing the lesson. Everything is in Divine timing. Spirit will decide when you are ready for more information or a new lesson.

While writing my book, I kept getting nudges from Spirit that I needed a psychic reading. A nudge from the spirit world is a gentle way to get your attention. It might seem to you like it is just you thinking about something. With practice, you can distinguish between your thoughts and spiritual messages. For me, when the nudge persists, I realize it is a message from Spirit, especially if the message was unexpected.

The nudges persisted, but I ignored them for a few weeks since nothing was troubling me. After almost convincing myself that I didn't need to connect with a psychic, a friend from Oaxaca called me, raving about a psychic reading she had from a woman traveling in Mexico.

I told her, "After I started writing this book, I sensed I needed to have a psychic reading. Just this week, I thought perhaps I had imagined that Spirit wanted me to connect with a psychic. Now, here you are out of the blue, telling me about this psychic."

"She is fantastic—the best psychic reading I ever experienced."

So, I switched gears and quit trying to convince myself that I did not need a psychic reading.

The psychic was an Asian woman who had been living in Chiapas, Mexico. We did a remote session. She explained she would be in a trance state. Afterward, I could ask her questions.

She quickly got into a trance state, and the session began. The information flowed through her with ease.

What an interesting and informative reading! Several things were extraordinary. She saw the octopus and the mermaid and merman energy almost immediately. That grabbed my attention; I had only had them for a couple of weeks. Many things she told me I already knew, but it was nice to receive confirmation.

Highlights of the psychic reading – things I already knew

- Lots of information is coming into my crown chakra, the energy point above your head that connects to the Divine.

- I am highly psychic and can easily see and experience things beyond the ordinary realms of awareness.

- My sacral chakra, the energy center about midway below the belly button, is full of creative ideas; all of them are ready to go. The sacral chakra also works with your emotional well-being, self-expression, sensitivity, and sexuality.

- I easily astral travel to other dimensions and planets.

- As a shape-shifter, I can be whoever I want to be. Legend says shape-shifters can change their physical appearance at will. In this lifetime, I have not turned myself into another being; however, sometimes, people tell me my face is shape-shifting. I can also see other people's faces shape-shift. It is pretty amazing to be talking with someone, and observe their face morph into faces they had in other lifetimes.

- The psychic noticed my hesitancy and fear of writing this book. I won't be able to "hide" my authentic sacred self anymore.

- I am working with the entire planet, not just individual sessions with people.

I was surprised when she told me my healing frequency is off the charts. The psychic said it is so powerful that it is difficult to describe.

What she told me next was mind-altering. She saw a dark entity in my belly. She said the entity looked like a scorpion or spider and was affecting my throat and mouth energy. It keeps me using a filter rather than being in my truth. This dark energy makes me feel unseen, not appreciated or understood.

"This dark entity is affecting your spiritual gifts and abilities."

As an energy healer, I know that dark energy can cause physical, mental, emotional, and spiritual problems. The problems go away once you remove the dark energy. The psychic wasn't sure how to remove this dark entity from my belly. I trusted my Spirit Guides and Eduardo would help me.

As she talked, my Spirit Guides gave me a nudge that it was Roberto, the shaman I met in Ecuador, who placed the entity in my belly after the massacre in ancient Egypt. It was his way of protecting me so that there would not be a repeat of what happened in Egypt.

What the psychic told me next was even more astonishing.

"You are responsible for the safety of this Universe. Spirit anchored the idea of being safe inside of you."

That is a tremendous responsibility! Ever since I started recalling the ancient lifetime in Egypt, the idea of shouldering the responsibility for the world has been a constant. The Wise Ones' leaders sent us to heal this planet. I was in charge of our group, and the mission failed because a few people in our group betrayed and helped kill us.

When I started having visions in 2010 about the many upcoming worldwide disasters, I tried to figure out what I could do to help. My first thought ten years later, when I saw that the world was in the middle of a pandemic, was "What can I do?" There has always been an underlying, nagging awareness that somehow I should be able to do something. Yet, many times, my human side would discount it by saying, "You are just one person. What can you do?"

Although the thought of me accepting the responsibility for the safety of this universe is overwhelming, what the psychic saw and said affirmed to me, I have been on the right track. For the past twelve years, my meandering path has led me to this moment. Each was a step, building a staircase to save the world.

Still, the human part of me wonders if I can rise and meet the challenge. Thank goodness my spiritual side trusts the Divine implicitly. If they choose me to keep the Universe safe, I trust I will realize what to do when the time comes.

The psychic continued with more mind-blowing revelations.

"You can heal the world. However, you might disappear because it would take so much out of you to accomplish this task."

This was an enormous revelation. The psychic was not talking in abstract terms. She meant I could literally heal the entire world by myself, which seemed overwhelming to me. It took a while to digest. I accepted that if Spirit wants me to heal the world, my Guides will tell me how and when to do it.

As a spiritual being, I am much more than my body. When I die, I will leave my body behind, but my soul will continue. So, the possibility of disappearing does not scare me.

My mind jumped to the mechanics. How would I be able to heal the world by myself? Do I already possess the knowledge of how to do it? Or will they only reveal it to me when it is time to do something?

One thing I was certain about, if I could save the world, I would do it in a heartbeat!

Since I might disappear, I chose a few people I trusted and told them what might happen. I wanted someone who would explain everything to my son. And, in case I disappeared, I wanted a few people to be aware of what happened.

One person asked, "How will I be certain you're gone because of the healing? What if something bad happened to you?"

"Easy. If you notice things have shifted in the world in a good way, then my healing worked. If nothing has changed, then you need to send someone to look for me."

Later, I meditated on how and why Roberto put the entity in my belly. A prior past life regression revealed that during the ancient Egyptian massacre, Roberto didn't come back and look for our baby and me. I was so hurt. My Spirit Guides told me his putting this entity inside of me was his way of apologizing and protecting me in future lifetimes.

I had a shamanic session with Eduardo to get more clarity.

"Wow, Chloe. Your energy is amazing. This is the strongest I have ever felt from you. It is so strong; you could connect spiritually with the entire world right now."

The psychic told me that I could heal the world just a few days before this session with Eduardo. It astonished me that the first words he mentioned were that my energy was strong enough to reach the entire world.

Eduardo's next comment was even more astounding.

"Chloe, you are emitting Buddha energy right now. No, not just energy. You are Buddha."

What?! Eduardo is saying I am Buddha? Maybe he meant at that moment I was embodying Buddha?

It felt overwhelming and a little shocking to hear Eduardo say I was Buddha. Actually, it's difficult to even wrap my head around it. I questioned whether I was up to the challenge of emanating Buddha in this lifetime. Like most of the highly unusual spiritual things that have happened to me, I sat with it and surrendered to Spirit. I trust I will embrace and use my inner Buddha whenever necessary.

Still, I had questions. How do I embrace the power of my spiritual side without becoming out of balance? Can I stay grounded and humble?

Remember when I said it can be challenging to accept spiritual messages? Being told I was Buddha, and that I could spiritually reach the entire world at one time and heal the planet are the most breathtaking messages I have ever received.

Part of me wanted to shrink back and say that's impossible; this must be some kind of mistake. However, since I started remembering and meeting people from that ancient Egyptian life, I have had an underlying impression that I was being prepared for something big.

In the past, I have relied more on my masculine energy. In our society, we have typically equated power with masculinity, aggression, competitiveness, and measuring our worth through our material accomplishments and success. When I tap into my feminine energy, it is easier to embrace my power without throwing me off balance.

It still felt a little out there, even for me. Eduardo doesn't throw out these comments flippantly. In my three years of having sessions with Eduardo, he has never said these kinds of things to me.

I told him, "Everything you are saying is so interesting to me. One reason I wanted to talk with you is to discuss some things a psychic told me last week."

My ninety-seven-year-old mother had died a few days before my session with Eduardo. When I told him about the entity in my belly, it stunned me to hear what he had to say.

"You are correct. Roberto put it there to protect you. It had to stay there until this lifetime when your mother died. It left your body the minute your mother left her own body."

"I don't understand. How is my mother's death connected to this entity?"

"It had to stay to protect you. Now you are safe to be yourself, with all your powers, abilities, wisdom, and knowledge."

Wow! No wonder I still struggle sometimes with owning and revealing my power. That entity had been inside me for thousands of years. It stayed there as a constant reminder that it was not safe to be my authentic spiritual self. The entity didn't leave my body until mid-October 2020. It makes sense it takes time to get that conditioned response out of my system.

Eduardo checked in with the guides about the psychic's prophecy of me healing the world.

"She's right on both accounts. You have the ability, and yes, it could take everything out of you to heal the world. Don't worry now about how; just continue moving forward and listen to your guides. They will reveal everything to you at the right time. Right now, the Spirit Guides want you to know the book you are writing is part of healing the world."

Eduardo was quiet for a moment.

Then he said, "Wow, this is interesting. You are being invited to become a Spiritual Grandmother, a tradition from my ancestral lineage that honors Indigenous spiritual wise women. This is a tremendous honor."

This was a big deal to me and completely unexpected! Spiritual Grandmothers are Indigenous wise women—usually healers, shamans, or curanderas—who have been chosen to share their wisdom. I am not Indigenous in this lifetime, although I have been Indigenous in many other lives.

Many believe the spirit world chose certain people "in a time before time" to come together to help heal the world. When

I read the prophecy that it is time for the Spiritual Grandmothers to share everything, even their most sacred secrets, it made sense why I am being called to share my authentic truth right now.

I hesitated to talk about the invitation to become a Spiritual Grandmother. Now I am more comfortable accepting everything. Since Eduardo and the Spirit Guides keep telling me this book is part of healing the world, I knew I had to put everything in the book.

Eduardo told me, "The guides are giving me initiation instructions for you to follow if you decide to accept the invitation to become a Spiritual Grandmother. There will be two ceremonies for you to perform—one week before Dia de Los Muertos, and one week afterward."

To prepare for my initiation, I had someone come do a limpia cleanse to clear the energy in my apartment. Then I did the two ceremonies in nature, as Eduardo had instructed me. Just as he predicted, my entire life was transforming in a big way.

Chapter 18
Sacred Work

A few months after the initiation ceremonies to become a Spiritual Grandmother, I found out my place was being sold. The next day, I saw a beautiful colonial house for rent. They build colonial houses in Mexico around a large courtyard in the middle of the house. This house has six French doors that all open up to the courtyard. Plus glorious sunsets and lake views from the large rooftop terrace. I always wanted to live in a colonial house. In less than two weeks, my wish came true.

After getting settled in my new house, I noticed my dog, Zooey, would sit in front of the door to the laundry room, staring and barking. She wouldn't move from that spot for long periods of time.

A few days later, while sitting in the courtyard talking on the phone, I became altered. What a bizarre experience—within minutes, I felt so high that I had difficulty walking and talking. Although I could understand what my friend was saying, it became more challenging to respond as each minute passed.

Then I started having problems getting my mouth to form words. My mouth became extremely parched. Everything seemed to move in slow motion, yet the changes in my body were at warp speed.

Similar to an "out-of-body" or lucid dream experience, I observed myself in my body, realizing I was losing my physical abilities. My mind tried to understand what was occurring.

I thought, "Wow, this is so weird! I have not had alcohol or any other substance, yet it is like I am high. I know no one has been here who could have drugged me. What is happening?!"

The intensity and speed of being this altered made me realize that getting safely to my bedroom was more important than figuring out the reason this was occurring. I grabbed Zooey.

Although it was only 6 p.m., I was too high to do anything. I got into bed and lay there for hours on a potent trip. No hallucinations. Just steady, ongoing sensations of floating, being in another dimension, and not being in my body.

If I had never been high before, I think this would have scared me. I knew just to relax and lean into it.

Not sure what to expect next, I wondered if something was being downloaded to me. Spiritual downloads from other dimensions bring new information and messages. Sometimes you can understand the message as it is being downloaded. Other times, they will reveal it to you at a later time. You may notice newfound abilities or insights after receiving a spiritual download.

After around four hours, I was able to go to sleep.

I had also felt a little sick since I moved into this house. I feared maybe the MS was coming back. It was time for me to book another session with Eduardo. He always starts his session by asking what is going on in your life.

"Hola, Chloe. ¿Cómo estás?"

"Hola. I am worried that the MS is coming back. I have been feeling sick like I used to experience when it was active."

Eduardo asked, "What else is going on?"

I told him about the altering experience and how Zooey had been acting at the door in front of the laundry room.

I shared, "I think there are some spirits stuck in the laundry room."

Eduardo asked me to give him a few minutes to check in with his guides.

"Yes, there are three spirits trapped there. They asked your Spirit Guides to bring you to this house so you could free them. They made you sick to get your attention. I think one of them might be responsible for altering you that day."

"So I need to help these spirits leave the earth plane?"

"Yes. Your guides are giving me specific information on how to help the stuck spirits. First, you need to tell them you are going to help. Ask them how much time they need to prepare to leave. After that, you will need to do a special releasing ceremony in front of the door to the laundry room."

"Okay. I have helped trapped spirits before, so I am comfortable with this process."

Eduardo said, "The other reason they brought you to this house is for your spiritual work. The house will serve as a sacred ashram for you to finish writing your book."

Eduardo continued, "They built the house on a sacred site. You are being asked to do a special twelve-day ceremony to honor it. The people who used to live on this land always surrounded themselves with vibrant colors. Every day for twelve days, I want you to create a mandala out of brightly colored flowers, and place it in each room for twenty-four hours. So, you will make twelve flower mandalas to put in each area of the house. Save all the flowers from each day's mandala. At the end of the twelve days, you will sprinkle the flowers throughout your garden and plants."

Many spiritual practices use mandalas to help with focus, gain spiritual insights, and deepen meditation and trance experiences. The word *mandala* means "circle" in Sanskrit. Most mandalas include colorful, symmetric, geometric patterns.

After my conversation with Eduardo, I was once again sitting in my courtyard, having a phone conversation. At the same time as the last experience, I became altered. Same scenario—I grabbed my dog and went to my bedroom. Like the first time, I remained extremely altered for hours.

I still had not yet talked to the spirits. The next day, I visited the laundry room.

"I am here to help release you to the Light. How much time do you need to be ready to leave?"

They replied, "We can be ready in three days."

I answered, "Great. In the meantime, whoever is giving me the altered experiences needs to stop. If you intended it as a gift, thank you. But please be clear, do not do it again. I don't want to be that high."

The trapped spirits left on the third day after I talked with them. Zooey was no longer fixated on the laundry room. The energy in my house felt lighter.

Now it was time to make the flower mandalas. My favorite flower shop has huge, brightly colored bouquets for only $2.50. Tapping into my artistic energy, I loved making the flower mandalas with a beautiful combination of yellow, pink, blue, lavender, red, and white flowers. A handmade ceramic tray and wooden bowl held the mandalas. The energy shifted each day. After I had completed the twelve days of fresh mandalas, I used my rattle, feather, and sage to clear the entire property.

Then I settled back into writing this book. The courtyard became one of my favorite places to write. Plenty of sunshine, comfy chairs, a table, lots of flowering plants, and a beautiful fountain—a perfect writer's haven.

Chapter 19

The Millennial, Generation Z, and Alpha Connection

Not all spirit messages are obvious when you receive them. Sometimes Spirit Guides put ideas in your mind because they want you to sit with them. Or maybe it isn't time for you to receive the entire message.

I consider millennials and later generations an important part of the market for this book. Not fully understanding why, I always honor my Spirit Guides' messages, so I included them. Later, I found some interesting statistics.

- A significant number of millennials are seeking shamans (Refinery29. Sept. 2019).
- Ninety-four percent of millennials will spend at least $300 per month for self-development to improve their lives (Self-improvement industry statistics).

- Millennials are now the second strongest and largest population group (Pew Research, 2019).

- Based on a 2021 reading habits study, millennials read more books than any other generation, and Generation Zs increased their reading more than any other group during the pandemic (BookBaby Blog, Jan. 11, 2022).

I also found it interesting that most of the professionals I hired to critique this book were millennials. It was not my intention to choose only millennials; they just seemed like the best fit. Some had knowledge of mystical spirituality; others had none. Yet, all of them loved what they read!

More importantly, the person who encouraged me to write this book is a millennial. Every time I would give her a reason not to write it, she would counter with why the world needed me to write this book. She convinced me to do it with no expectations or concerns about the ultimate outcome; allowing it to be a beautiful opportunity to trust the Universe.

Several months later, I was talking to my son and shared that I wasn't clear why, but I thought millennials and the generations after them would be a significant part of the book's audience.

"Mom, many of my friends and I are having very weird spiritual things happen. This book will help us understand and let us know what to do. Your willingness to be so honest and reveal everything you've experienced will help other people who are having similar experiences."

Later that night, I had an "aha" moment.

Of course, they are an important market for my book. Many millennials, Generation Z and Alphas, came in as Star Children. Their soul's purpose is to help change and heal the world. My book can guide their continued spiritual awakening and show them how to recognize, embrace, and use their extraordinary abilities.

Many in the metaphysical world believe there are several groups of Star Children now on Earth. Most share some common attributes. They are empathic and skilled communicators with an enhanced ability to read energy. They are old souls, here to change and heal the world. Many are multitalented and active in the creative arts. Although they may seem impatient, that comes from their frustration about the world still being bogged down in old perceptions and ways of doing things.

From a young age, Star Children may wonder how they got here. It doesn't take long for them to realize how different they are than most of the population. Many can recall past lives. They bring memories, knowledge, and wisdom from other lives and dimensions to Earth. They love being in nature. Indigos came to challenge old ways so that the Crystals and Rainbows could accomplish their goals. Not everyone born during this time is a Star Child. The suggested years each type of Star Children were born is a guide. There can be crossovers; some may have several traits from more than one group, others might be born on the cusp with multiple traits.

Most Indigos were born between 1970 and 1994. They are change-makers. Sometimes the pressure and expectations they put upon themselves because they are aware they came to Earth to make changes can create problems in their relationships with others. Without understanding why or how, they are highly psychic. It can be a struggle for an Indigo to comply with authority and rules. They are not afraid to stand up for their principles. Like the other Star Children, they embody wisdom beyond their years. It is possible that many Indigos came to Earth after World War II and then again from the 1970s to the 1990s. So, if you were born between 1950 and 1994, you might be an Indigo.

Most Crystals were born during 1995–2012. They are usually calm, loving, and forgiving. Some Crystals prefer communicating telepathically or through music. Many are on the autistic spectrum. Crystals allow their hearts to guide them; they lead with love and peace. Highly empathic and intuitive, many Crystals are natural healers and spiritual teachers. Good at creating miracles, they carry an extremely high vibration and are like a wise sage. Their goal is to heal the shadow side of the world.

Rainbows were born in 2012 and later. These children are born truth-tellers with balanced male and female energy. Serene and wise, this is usually the first time they have lived on Earth. Rainbows are here to heal and realign our world and can be strong-willed in accomplishing their mission. Gifted with claircognizance (sensing things beyond the physical senses), they embrace their spiritual side and are not concerned with fitting in with the general population. When you meet a Rainbow, you will marvel at their wisdom and gifts. They are empathic, somewhat quirky, and can be shy.

Do you need a spiritual mentor?

When you are born with spiritual gifts and ancient wisdom, you may feel bewildered. I didn't understand why I was with my family; they were so different from me. Even as a young child, I was aware that I wasn't the same as most people. When you look around and wonder where your peeps are because you can't find anyone on your level, it can be lonely and confusing.

I wish someone had guided me spiritually when I was younger. Instead, I had to figure out most things on my own. It would've been so much easier with a mentor shining a light on the bigger reason I was here.

So, my dear Star peeps, I am here to help guide you with your reawakening, your spiritual purpose, and your mission to realign and heal the world. The spiritual world is a magnificent, miraculous place that offers answers and solutions to make our world a better place. My goal is to guide as many people as possible to awaken to the power of the Universe, help heal the world, and find and embrace your soul's Divine path and purpose.

Do you remember when the students of Marjory Stoneman Douglas High School in Parkland, Florida, spoke out about the tragic shootings at their school? Many accused them of being actors because they thought it was impossible for young people to be so articulate. I suspect many of them are Star Children. As I listened to them, it was the first time in a long time that I felt hope for our world's future. It was very frustrating to see adults attacking and trying to discredit these kids. I am sure it was difficult for the students to keep up their momentum while they were being bombarded with so much negative energy.

I also suspect Greta Thunberg, born in 2003, is a Crystal. She started holding large protests against climate change when she was fifteen years old. These young people do not care what others think about them. They are comfortable speaking their minds. Star people have an inner knowing that they are being called to take action, to lead our world in a new direction.

Our world needs more brave souls to stand up, speak out, and do the legwork to make lasting changes. We are at a tipping point. Are we going to rise, awaken, and empower others? The spirit world has been trying to get our attention. If enough people don't wake up, the world as we know it will end. Which side of history do you want to be on?

Chapter 20

Finding Your Intuitive Voice

———— ୭୭୧ ————

The dictionary defines *intuition* as "knowledge from an ability to understand or know something based on your feelings rather than facts." For those of you who lead with your head and accept nothing unless they back it with logic and scientific proof, it's difficult to surrender to your intuitive thoughts.

Although I was open, and not bogged down with needing logic and scientific proof, I spent years claiming my intuitive thoughts were just a series of coincidences. In my early fifties, I identified patterns and answers about why and when I experienced problems. Guess what?! Any time my inner voice warned me about something, and I didn't honor the warning, bad things happened. I was so struck by this revelation that I got my first tattoo, the Chinese symbol for "Trust Truth." The tattoo artist put it on my belly to have a visual reminder to trust my intuition.

"These thoughts just came up out of nowhere. How can they be right?"

I suggest getting quiet and checking in with yourself. Be a diligent observer. How does your body feel when you receive an intuitive message? What does your heart say? Breathe the intuitive thoughts in and exhale your doubts. In the beginning, don't worry if they are right. This is the time for small steps. Decide you are open to receiving more messages.

Maybe I am just daydreaming. How can I trust something that seems so random?

Gaining solid trust in your intuition takes time. You can't force it. When you are ready for your next step, start keeping a journal of your most significant intuitive thoughts. Check back to reread your journal notes to identify if any of your intuitive messages come true.

How can I better understand what my intuition is trying to tell me?

This takes practice. The indirect messages can be difficult to recognize. Sometimes if I miss a message, it keeps coming back until I can interpret it correctly. I had a recent experience where I resisted what my intuition was trying to tell me. I met with a new friend several times. Both times I was sick the next day like I used to feel when I had multiple sclerosis. Wanting this budding friendship to continue, I ignored my intuition and decided it was just a coincidence. However, I made a promise to myself that if it happened after the third time, I could no longer pretend it was just a coincidence.

I was sick again the next day after we were together. All three times were the same. I would feel MS-sick for the entire next day, waking up the following morning fine. When I accepted my intuition about this situation, what struck me was the connection to multiple sclerosis. Many of my alternative remedies to get rid of MS showed me that Spirit was using it as a powerful way to get my attention.

How can I access my intuition?

We are all surrounded by spiritual helpers. They don't interfere or intervene unless they are aware you want help. Talk to them. Tell them you want them in your life. Rather than asking your guides to help, start by thanking them for being with you and offering their guidance. Let them know how much you appreciate their help.

I try to avoid asking for help because that can imply you are uncertain you will receive it. I prefer stating, "Thank you for your help." It is a subtle but important difference. So, instead of asking my Spirit Guides, "Can you help me with writing this book?" I say, "Thank you so much for helping me write my book. I appreciate your guidance, insight, and gentle nudges on what is important to include in the book."

Is intuition as important as other spiritual abilities?

Honoring and encouraging your intuition unlocks the door to more spiritual tools. Spiritual awakening builds from each step you take. The more you are able and willing to embrace the tools, the more you will receive.

It is a wonderful lesson in manifestation. When Spirit sees you are trying to live an authentic spiritual life, you will receive more help. If I get a bit off-track and bogged down with everyday life, all I need to do is refocus on my spiritual life, and intuitive messages surround me like a warm hug.

Should I focus first on honing my intuitive skills?

For me, intuition was one of the easiest spiritual tools I used. First, try to release your doubts. Become an open vessel for receiving messages and guidance. Try to resist naming your intuition as just coincidence. If you have resistance, try thinking of it as a game. Approach it with curiosity. "Hmm … maybe what didn't seem to make sense will become clear to me at a later point in time."

I remember one semester living in a dorm. There was only one phone per floor. My dorm room was right next to the phone booth. The only times I answered it, the call was always for me. I wondered if I could tell when someone was calling me. But I never mentioned this to anyone because it seemed a little too "out there" for me to admit. Now it happens all the time. Right before someone calls or texts me, I receive a flash of them in my mind. It has happened so many times with my son that he knows the first words out of my mouth will be, "I was just thinking about you."

How do I know my intuitive thoughts are from the Divine?

That's a tricky one. Just because you can intellectually understand a concept doesn't mean you embody it emotionally. For me, there was a magical shift from my head to my heart, and I no longer had doubts about my intuition. Yes, I still have times when I resist what my intuition is trying to tell me. The difference is that I do not doubt my intuition but sometimes linger in magical thinking, wishing that my intuition wasn't right.

Recently, I had a powerful reminder of what happens when you ignore your intuitive guidance. I took a brief road trip and planned on being gone for a week. It started raining the night before I left, so I decided it would be a good idea to pull my plants out and let them have a good soak. I received an intuitive message that I would slip and fall. I thought the danger would be if I hit my head on the concrete. So, I told myself that I would be very careful. As I walked back into the house, I slipped and fell. Relieved that I didn't hit my head, I reached to pull myself up. That's when I saw it—my middle toe was twisted into a weird shape and was already bruising and swelling. I was focusing on not hurting my head; instead, I broke my toe.

Waiting for clarity from your intuition can take a great deal of patience. Everything is in Divine time, not your timetable. I made the trip with my broken toe because I needed to figure out if it was the right time to move to San Miguel de Allende. For the first four days, I was excited about moving. On the fourth evening, as I was going to check out an apartment rental, it surprised me to receive a very strong intuitive message to not move. When I asked for more clarity, I was told that I might move there later, but not now.

Part of me, my magical thinker, wanted to pretend that this wasn't intuitive guidance. I had lived in San Miguel de Allende before and loved it; I wanted to make this work. And that is a red flag—when you continue trying to make something work after they have guided you to stop. That was one of the powerful signs for me; I realized I was trying too hard to make this move work. Then I reminded myself of my broken toe that I could have avoided if I had heeded my intuitive guidance. You may not like what your intuition is telling you. Trust it anyway. Your intuition is always directing you to your highest good.

Nurture your intuition

Practice using all of your senses. Be open to all forms of communication. An intuitive idea or message can present itself through various channels. Many times when I am talking with people, something they say grabs my attention. I make a mental note to remember and meditate or pray about it. Sometimes I receive clarity quickly; other times, it may take weeks.

Stay present to your environment. I have received intuitive messages from music, books, TV, movies, videos, nature, social media, dreams, animals, my body—Spirit will try whatever is necessary to get your attention. Do your best not to discount the messages as random thoughts or only your imagination.

Intuition is your link to the Divine. Allow yourself to be open to receiving. Trust the more you embrace the Divine, the more will be revealed to you.

Ways to harness your intuition

Meditate

In the beginning, don't get caught up in what type of meditation you use; the important thing is to do it regularly. Experiment with different meditations until you find what resonates with you. Sometimes guided meditation is the perfect thing for me. Other times, I might listen to sacred music like kirtan or shamanic drumming and let the music take me on a journey. For walking meditation, it is best to be in nature. Freestyle dancing can be a wonderful movement meditation. Singing, chanting, or playing an instrument are also ways to tap into a meditative state.

Physical exercise

Sometimes in a yoga class, when I go into a deep meditation, it takes a while for me to come back to the room. Other good choices are tai chi (a slow-moving, graceful exercise, created as a self-defense martial art, and used for relaxation, stress reduction, and other health conditions) and qigong (series of body postures and movement, breathing and meditation, enhancing your health, spirituality, and martial arts practice).

Dreams

Many of my intuitive messages come through dreams. In the dream world, your conscious mind does not override your subconscious. Thank your Spirit Guides for talking to you through your dreams. To kick start your connection with your guides, give them something specific that you would like help with before going to sleep.

I remember a vision dream I had in my twenties. It was a long and detailed dream about my boyfriend cheating on me with his old girlfriend. When I woke up, I did my best to convince myself it was just a random dream. Imagine my surprise when I found out everything I saw in my dream was exactly what happened between my boyfriend and the old girlfriend.

Another intuitive boyfriend message wasn't in a dream but came as a direct message. As soon as I woke up, I had a powerful message with these simple words, "It's over." It seemed strange. We had not fought. The last time we were together, everything was fine. But the message was so clear. I knew to be prepared that it was over.

Use tools to help train your intuition

I prefer to use direct communication with my Spirit Guides. But many also use other tools to receive and understand intuitive messages. When trying to find your intuitive voice, it can be helpful to use extra tools, like oracle cards or a pendulum. First, listen and observe what your intuition is trying to tell you. Then you can test yourself by pulling a card or swinging a pendulum to check if you get a similar answer.

Oracle cards provide insight and guidance. You can pull one card, perhaps asking a question like, "What do I need to focus on today?" Most oracle card guidebooks include different ways to pull cards and interpret the messages. I like to pull three cards, using the first card to represent the past, the second card for the present, and the third card for the future. When you use the oracle cards as a guide for strengthening your intuitive skills, first meditate on your questions and develop your intuitive messages before reading the oracle cards.

With my angel cards, I don't depend on them for major guidance but sometimes enjoy pulling them. I use them more like an affirmation to focus on the words for that day.

I also have a deck of oracle cards. Like the angel cards, I don't depend on them but appreciate getting a glimpse of the energy that is surrounding me.

For me, using extra tools is only one piece of the puzzle. My goal is to receive my Spirit Guide messages directly. Whenever I get a psychic reading, I want a reader who doesn't use tools. When I do my healing work with others, it is always straight from the source; I don't rely on other tools to give me answers.

Broaden your world

Take a different route to work, go on a retreat, have a no-plans spontaneous day, get out of your comfort zone, try new things, travel. These can help you get out of autopilot and hear your intuition better. My son and I had a game when he was little. We called it "let's take a vacation day." The rule was we had to leave our house early. The first stop was going to eat breakfast. We took turns choosing what activity to do next. The other rule was we could not go home until it was bedtime. It was so much fun to shake up our routine.

Be mindful and present

If you remain in the moment, your mind quiets down, giving you a better chance of connecting with your intuition.

Trust your imagination

When I attended a workshop for doing psychic readings, one of the most valuable things I learned was to be open to everything you see and hear during a session. It's okay if you think it is just your imagination. You can always check back later and find out if anything was correct.

Engage in creative projects

Bring more creativity into your life. When you immerse yourself in a project, it is like meditating. Once you are in the creative zone, things flow more freely, and you are more in tune with insights and messages.

Relax

Take a long soak in the tub. Many of my "aha" moments come to me when I take a bath. I like to fill my tub with essential oils, rose petals, Epsom salts, sea salt, and organic bubble bath.

Intuitive messages

Intuition speaks to us on many levels. You might have a quick vision flash. Other times, a more comprehensive vision is like watching a movie. Hunches or gut feelings are common. Many experience physical sensations like goosebumps. Tiny tears of joy appear when I am in the presence of the Divine, confirming to me I am on the right path.

When beings visit me in spirit form, I am cognizant of their energy. First, I have an awareness that someone is there. Since I can see spirits, I look around the room, asking, "Who is here?" I may have to repeat that question several times before I am clear who is there with me. Sometimes I don't get any clarity and trust that it is not time for that spirit to be revealed to me.

I use the same process when I am doing an energy healing session. Before beginning, the client and I set our intention and express our gratitude. I always explain that it is up to Spirit whether a past life will come up in the session. If I notice we have stepped into a past life, I ask questions.

"Where are we?"

"Who is here with us?"

"What do we need to learn about this lifetime?"

While asking these questions, I scan with my third eye to gather more information. At some point, everything unfolds, like I am watching a movie.

I encourage you to practice your intuitive skills. They open so many amazing spiritual doors.

Chapter 21

Creating a Regular Spiritual Practice

---––⁊ʔ⁊ɕ───---

Through trial and error, I have found what works well for me. I only keep the practices I resonate with that help me stay grounded and focused on my spirituality. My goal is to "walk my talk" rather than adhere to other people's views and beliefs.

My day begins with a prayer while I light a candle and incense. It is a lovely way to greet the day, engage your senses, and set your intentions.

The prayer can be short and simple: "Thank you for this new day."

You can add more wording:

"Thank you for removing anything that is blocking me from becoming my authentic spiritual self, with all my knowledge, wisdom, power, and abilities. Thank you for restoring my mind, body, spirit, and space to their optimal functioning, in all ways, all dimensions, all times, and all realities."

Or create wording to deal with whatever is happening in your life. The point is to set the tone for your day by expressing your gratitude. Create a prayer that reflects your priorities and spiritual purpose.

I love to acknowledge other times, realities, and dimensions in my prayers. When you are talking or praying to Spirit, it is best to be clear. If you are only asking for help in your current lifetime, you could leave or bring negative energy from other dimensions and lives. For example, when I visualized the multiple sclerosis being removed, I wanted it gone in all ways, times, realities, and dimensions. I don't want MS ever showing up again in my energy field.

Sacred music

Determine what sounds call to your soul. My favorite sacred music is kirtan, crystal bowls, and percussion. I am also drawn to world music, especially Middle Eastern and African. Make some playlists of music that connect you with your spirituality. Music is playing in my house from early morning until bedtime. It is a constant yet subtle reminder to my psyche to live my life as a spiritual being.

I like to set the tone for the day by starting with kirtan or crystal bowl music. As the day progresses, I add lots of percussion music, especially when I want to increase my energy. I switch to something a little calmer toward late afternoon, like Kora Chill, hang drum, or cello music.

Meditation

I recommend daily meditation. It is easy to access apps, videos, and classes. Some common types of meditation:

- **Breathwork** – focuses on your breath. A simple one to try is Dr. Andrew Weil's 4-7-8 breathing method. First, empty your lungs. Then, inhale slowly through your nose for four seconds. For the next seven seconds, hold your inhaled breath. During the last eight seconds, exhale through your mouth. You can do this up to four times.

- **Focus** – pick an item to focus on while you meditate. Candles can engage both your visual and olfactory senses. Concentrate on seeing only the candle; notice all the little details, like how the flame flickers or how it smells if you used a scented candle.

- **Mantra** – repeating of a word or phrase, silently or out loud.

- **Transcendental Meditation (TM)** – introduced by Maharishi Mahesh Yogi, it uses a mantra, which you continuously repeat to yourself while meditating. It's suggested you do fifteen to twenty-minute sessions twice a day.

- **Mindfulness meditation** – giving whatever you are doing 100 percent of your attention. Focus only on the present moment; there are no thoughts of the past or future. You can do this anytime, or while doing a simple activity like washing dishes.

- **Muscle relaxation** – tightening and releasing muscles throughout the body. My favorite version of this is yoga nidra.

- **Physical mindfulness** – walking, dancing, creating art, singing and exercise are all ways to incorporate meditation in your life.

- **Guided meditation** – can be an easier way to get used to meditating. All you need to do is get comfortable and focus on what the person leading the meditation is saying.

- **Zen meditation** – comes from the Buddhist Mahayana tradition. In this process, you are the observer of your thoughts. Notice them when they come up, and then let them go.

Make an altar

Raised as a Methodist and later Episcopalian, I converted to Judaism as an adult. It took me a while to be okay with having an altar at my house. In most organized religions, they worship items placed on an altar. I didn't want to worship or pray to items. Instead, I use my altar as a visual reminder to live a spiritual life. Now, even when I travel, I bring mini altars with me.

Start by thinking about what is important to you spiritually. Those are the things you want to have on your altar. The colonial house I rented in Mexico is large and spread out, so I created three altars. The living room altar has replicas of my spirit animals—the dragonfly, jaguar, snake, and hummingbird. It also has a seashell from Peru, various crystals, feathers, sage, hearts, a handmade copper mug I use with ceremonies, a beautiful indigenous shaker, and a seashell a friend brought me from the beach in Zihuatanejo. On the kitchen altar, you will find more spirit animals, hearts, candles, a rattle, and my angel cards. In the bedroom, there are reminders from spiritual healings, powerful stones and crystals, a lock of my soul dog, Gordito's, hair, his paw imprint, and more seashells.

I often stop what I am doing to look at the altar. Or I might go over and hold an item in my hand, breathing in its energy. It helps me be mindful of how important my spirituality is to me.

Engage your senses

Besides lighting incense in the mornings, I like to burn it throughout the day. I am also a big fan of aromatherapy with essential oils and have two diffusers in my house. I can see multiple spiritual items in every room of my house. In the living room, where I spend much of my time, I have a flying primitive wooden angel hanging in one window. Buddhist tapestries adorn the dining room and kitchen walls. You will find hearts or angels in every room. When I need to heighten my sense of touch, I hold one of my spiritual items and visualize its energy pulsating throughout my body. Whenever I do a ceremony or want to connect with my sense of taste, I make a special drink using cacao, roasted blue corn, fresh cinnamon, ground parsley, and honey.

Journaling

As you continue on your journey of spiritual awakening, it is helpful to write down your thoughts, progress, gratitude, questions, and experiences. First, writing about them takes it out of your head. It is an easy way to empty your mind and get back to the moment. Looking through your journal gives you a big-picture view of your journey. It is helpful to review where you've been and where you are going. You can see and acknowledge your progress, make a note of where to get additional help for a particular problem or highlight something that worked well.

Seek guidance

I am a big believer that spiritual awakening and healing are a team effort. My intuition lets me know when I need to work with someone, read a book, take a class, view a video, or attend a webinar. At the start of my reawakening journey, I did all of those with greater frequency than I do now. Everything was so new; I wanted to dive right in, surround myself with knowledge, wisdom, and garner new abilities.

You will find spiritual healing and awakening intertwined. When you go to a healer, it is likely that the session will also address spiritual awakening issues. Or you see someone for awakening guidance, and you realize healing has also taken place.

After my Mexican shaman, Eduardo, told me I would go through a major transformation, Spirit Guides started speaking to me through Eduardo during our sessions. A Mayan Spirit Guide showed up to make sure I remained focused on writing this book. Eduardo and the guides have communicated there is an urgency to get my book out as quickly as possible to help others understand how spirituality is connected to what is happening in our world.

When your energy connects deeply with another person's energy, it is a gift from Spirit. Pay attention to those relationships. I know and trust Eduardo to give me the messages I need at the right time.

Daily reading

I have committed to daily readings every morning. Books are splendid, but not very practical when you travel a lot. Here are three online sites that I regularly use for inspiration and spiritual connection.

- **www.dailyom.com** – sends inspiring short essays five days a week. They also offer some great online courses.

- **www.tut.com** – sends uplifting and humorous spiritual messages on weekdays. They also offer remote and physical classes, events, and videos.

- **www.leeharrisenergy.com** – Lee is a shamanic intuitive energy guide, teacher, musician; he channels his guides, The Z's. He also offers classes, webinars, music, and videos.

Check in with your intuition about spiritual subjects to study

In my twenties, I read about chakras, which are energy points in your body that help regulate your physical, emotional, mental, and spiritual systems. After moving to Asheville, it drew me to learn more about them. First, I took a simple seven-week course. We focused on one chakra per class. Before each class was over, we discussed how that chakra shows up in our lives. One woman in the class never talked. She finally said something on the fifth chakra, which is in the throat and is all about communication. She talked for quite a while. It was fascinating to see and hear her talk. Something about that chakra struck a chord in her, and the floodgates opened. It inspired me to start writing a play about chakras.

Later, when I started doing energy healing work, the chakras became important to my work. They make sense to me. During my healing sessions, I am always processing through the chakras, clearing, balancing, and strengthening them for my clients.

Chakras are a big part of my life. In the mornings, I do a short meditation check-in on which chakra colors I need to surround myself with for the day. Once I choose my clothes, I ask if I need to wear more of a particular color. I might need to add a particular scarf, bag, sweater, or jewelry to help with my chakra needs.

If I am a little off, I check to see which chakra is out of alignment or needs extra attention. Chakras are like a blueprint for understanding yourself better. For me, they provide an internal map for healing myself and others.

My experience with the chakras is a great example of trusting your intuition. When I took the chakra class, I did not know it would lead me to write a play or become an energy healer for others. It is okay not to know everything all at once. Open up to new experiences and see where they lead you.

Commit to your spiritual growth

Vow that you will do at least one thing to enhance your spiritual life every day. Small steps are fine. Continue adding more to your daily practice. Soon it will become second nature to look and live in the world through spiritual eyes.

Be mindful of how and with whom you spend your energy

- Limit the time you spend watching or reading the news.
- Fill your life with positive, uplifting activities and people.
- If you feel drained, weak, or sick after spending time with certain people, it might be a good idea to limit how much time you spend with them.

Chapter 22

Understanding Your Spiritual Awakening

———— ༄ ༄ ༄ ————

A spiritual awakening can happen quickly or might take years. Having been interested in spirituality and metaphysics since high school, I considered myself a seeker. I had no goal of becoming "spiritually awakened"—but wanted to find out how others create healthy, happy lives.

I remember being mesmerized by the book *Siddhartha* when I was a teenager. In 1922, Hermann Hesse wrote this novel about a journey of self-discovery and transformation a young man, Siddhartha, experienced. He abandons his wealthy life to find spiritual enlightenment.

Even though I didn't decide to seek an awakening, the book had a profound effect on broadening my horizons. The idea of having a spiritual path different from my religious background appealed to me. The book planted a beautiful seed in my mind about other paths one can take to find spiritual fulfillment.

Another thing I experienced as a teen that opened my eyes to other dimensions was an LSD trip I took in San Francisco. Picture 1969, the Summer of Love. A free-spirited seventeen-year-old long-haired hippie girl, trying a hallucinogenic for the first time.

My step-sister, who lived in Haight Ashbury, had a friend of hers accompany me to keep me safe. After I took it, we headed to Golden Gate Park. I always loved spending time there. With the LSD magnifying and enhancing everything, the park was glorious. We visited all my favorite Golden Gate Park haunts— the Japanese Tea Garden, the buffalos, botanical gardens, and lying on the grass, basking in the sun.

Noticing a lot of activity at the museum, we walked over. Upon entering the building, I saw they had set up a large two-story white wall as a viewing screen. By now, the LSD effects were powerful.

The screening started. OMG! It was a live feed of the U.S. astronauts walking on the moon! I can't describe what an extraordinary experience it was to be tripping on LSD in Golden Gate Park while I watched the live stream of men walking on the moon. What an amazing experience and memory. It was a moment of taking in the Universe's vastness; Earth is only one small part of it.

Later, I decided to go to the Esalen Institute in Big Sur, California. My "chaperone" wanted us to take the bus. It was a beautiful night on Highway One coastal road.

I said, "No way. It is too beautiful to be cooped up on a bus. Let's hitchhike."

My step-sister had picked one of her most conservative friends to be with me. Not the type of person to embrace the idea of hitchhiking.

"I think we should take the bus. It will be safer."

I answered, "You can take the bus. But I am going to hitchhike."

Since he promised to keep me safe, he reluctantly followed me to the highway. In no time, we had a ride.

The car was full of musicians. I remember sitting in the front seat, which gave me a perfect view of this gorgeous drive—mountains on one side and the Pacific Ocean on the other side. They had great music blasting on the radio. Everything felt magical. I didn't just hear the music; I could see colors from the music while it danced around me. The ocean, the trees, plants, birds, and animals were alive, dancing and pulsating in unison with the music.

I had a distinct moment of realizing there is so much more in our universe than we experience with our regular five senses. I became one with the Universe, connecting with everything. The limited third dimension reality dropped its curtain. We are not the only planet, civilization, or people in the Universe; we are just one small part.

When we arrived at the Esalen Institute around 2 a.m., I was still high. The next morning, it delighted me to see they were having a musical concert on the cliffs overlooking the Pacific Ocean. There were some famous musicians, like Ravi Shankar, playing. Lying back on the grass, basking in the sun's warmth covering my body, I closed my eyes and breathed in this entire experience—the music, the sound of the waves as they hit the cliffs, the sun caressing my body. I could not have asked for a more perfect ending to my LSD experience.

I am not sharing this LSD story to glorify drugs or encourage you to have a hallucinogenic experience. Nor am I suggesting you hitchhike, something I would never do now. In fact, it surprised me when Spirit suggested putting it in the book. My goal is to be as transparent as possible about sharing my awakening experiences.

When Spirit asked me to think back through my life about anything that opened or enhanced my awareness, this story popped up. You can get to the same altered state with natural methods, like meditation and chanting. My recommendation is for people to use natural methods for a spiritual awakening.

My awakening journey has been a slow process. It introduced me to many new ideas. Some I embraced; others I filed away to revisit later.

My curiosity and willingness to try new things kept me on my awakening path. Your experience may differ from mine. Maybe you make a conscious commitment to awaken and start adding activities to make it happen. You might read books, take webinars or classes, start a regular spiritual practice, seek healers and spiritual teachers. I did all those things, but over a thirty-year period. Content to wait for Divine timing, I was not rushing to make anything happen.

I have no regrets about how my journey unfolded. In 2007, when I moved to Asheville, North Carolina, my spiritual journey went into warp speed. I realized something significant was happening and leaned into it. From the moment I breathed in a past life partner's breath in 2008, recognizing I knew him from the "time before time" and remembering every spiritual experience I had in this life in a matter of seconds, I knew my life would never be the same.

What matters the most is that you remain open. Anyone can have a spiritual awakening. Some may be quick. For others like me, it can take years. Choose to awaken, and Spirit will show up to help you.

If you have experiences that confuse or scare you, reach out for guidance

First, I tried talking to my spiritual friends in Asheville about all the wisdom and abilities appearing in my life. It shocked and confused me when they said they had not had these experiences. Feeling lost for a while, I accepted spiritual things were opening up for me in a big way.

I remember a poignant conversation I had with a friend during this time of accelerated spiritual growth.

"Chloe, you are giving your power away when you assume all these spiritual gifts you are receiving are because of other people."

"What do you mean?"

"When you told me Micah's Soul Body was showing up at your house, you presumed he was the one making it happen."

"Yes, that's true. I have never seen a Soul Body in this lifetime. So, unless it is him causing it to happen, how could I be doing it? It has never happened to me until after I met him."

"Yes, dear one, I understand. I am just saying if you can imagine Micah is sending his Soul Body to you, why not imagine you are the one who is bringing it to you?"

It took me years to accept it was me bringing the Soul Bodies.

Trust the process. Have faith everything will be revealed to you at the right time. Commit to your awakening and help others wake up. Everything else will fall into place.

One professional who read the early drafts of this book said he identified three major themes of my book: faith, trust, and acceptance. They all work together.

Learn to trust that everything happens in Divine timing. Accept that meanings, understandings, and answers will come when the time is right. It is okay not to understand everything. Embrace your faith to carry on. Let things unfold naturally. Allow yourself to flow with the energy of the Universe.

Chapter 23

Starting Your Healing Spiritual Journey

―――――――――⟋ᔕᔐᔑ⟍―――――――――

You don't need to do everything at once. It is okay to start small and go slow.

First, I suggest identifying any problems you are experiencing—physically, mentally, emotionally, and spiritually. Then determine which areas seem most problematic.

I. What are the problem areas of my life? Please rate on a scale of 1 to 5 (1 being a minor problem; 5 a big problem).

- PHYSICALLY

- EMOTIONALLY

- MENTALLY

- SPIRITUALLY

II. Begin with the areas with the highest numbers, and go through this process with each area.

- Would some alternative healing help?
- What type of alternative healing is best for this problem?
- Am I drawn to a special type of healing?
- Do I need any Western medical approaches for this problem?

Many times, especially if this is new to you, it is wise to start out by seeing a Western medical doctor to get more clarity about what is happening. You can still use alternative healing as a complement to your medical doctor's suggestions. In fact, if I think I might have a serious medical problem, that is my approach. When my doctor thought I had uterine and ovarian cancer, I combined my approach with Western medicine and alternative healing.

- Would some spiritual guidance help with this problem?

III. After you identify the problem area you want to work on, research what healing helps with the problem.

- Ask people who are open to alternative healing which healing therapists and modalities they have used.
- Search for online recommendations.
- Contact alternative healing therapists and/or doctors, and ask them to give you an idea of how they work, what process they use, what types of healing they include, and what type of success they experience when dealing with

the problems you are having. As you talk and listen to them, pay attention to their energy.

After narrowing down your choice, schedule an appointment. Go with an open mind. Meditate before your appointment to clear and relax your mind. Remain open to healing.

IV. Observe how you feel during the healing session.

- If they do hands-on healing, are their hands hot to you? In my experience, the hotter their hands, the better.

- What are you experiencing emotionally while they work on you?

- Was it easy to get to a relaxed state?

- Are you getting an intuitive "Yes" that something is shifting?

- Are you experiencing any profound spiritual messages, for example, remembering a past life that could affect your problem in this life? Did you see or hear visitors from other dimensions or receive guidance from Spirit Guides?

- Are you experiencing any physical sensations?

- Is there a connection between you and the healer? Are you on a similar wavelength? Is the conversation flowing well between you and the healer?

V. After the session.

Take some deep breaths, and notice if anything is different. Check in with all areas—physically, emotionally, mentally, and spiritually.

Overall, was it a positive experience? For me, as long as it was not a negative experience, I will try at least three sessions before I decide if that healer becomes a part of my regular healing team. You should be able to see some noticeable progress in three sessions.

I have used alternative healing for over fifty years. There were plenty of alternative therapies that did not work for me; that doesn't mean they aren't effective or won't work for someone else. It just means that it was not a good fit for me.

Create your healing team

I suggest finding healers for each area of your life. As your intuition strengthens, you will get more guidance on what type of healers you need. For me, I must be able to connect deeply with my healers. I want us to work as a team, where we honor and combine our spiritual abilities, knowledge, wisdom, and spiritual guidance to achieve lasting healing.

When I travel to other countries, my priority is to work with local healers and healing traditions. My first choice will always be an Indigenous healer. There is something quite magical about receiving healing from someone who is native to the area and uses healing traditions that have been around for hundreds or thousands of years.

Do you need a spiritual teacher?

I am not one to follow a particular spiritual path or dogma. For both my healing work and my spiritual journey, my Spirit Guides and my intuition lead my path. When something resonates with me, I continue exploring it. Once it doesn't resonate with me anymore, I discontinue it.

My preference is to learn things independently rather than have a specific spiritual teacher. I choose not to depend on a guru; I don't believe or practice putting people on a pedestal and letting them serve as my connection to the Divine. Everyone can have a personal, beautiful relationship with the Divine. You don't need another person to be your spiritual voice; you can talk directly to the Divine.

The idea of the student becoming the teacher and the teacher becoming the student drives home the fluidness of a spiritual healing journey. We are like pieces of a puzzle; what we contribute is just as important as what others share. I want to work with people who understand that all puzzle pieces have value.

If you decide to get a spiritual teacher, I suggest you use the same diligence you used to find your healers. Research. Read. Take part in introductory webinars and courses. Ask for recommendations. As you learn more about a particular spiritual teacher, make a note of how you feel about them, their thoughts, their teachings ... and always permit yourself to try a different path if it doesn't resonate with you.

Understanding your journey is an ongoing process. I encourage you to get a journal to capture your thoughts and experiences. At times, something will happen that seems random and not connected to anything else in your life. Make a note of it; Spirit will give you more information at a later time. Many times my "aha" moments come years later.

If you are uncomfortable with relying on alternative healing, start small. Pick one alternative healing method to try as a complement to more traditional methods. I prefer working with healers who respect when it is necessary to use Western medicine. Although my preference is natural healing methods, I remain open to what my body needs.

With my plantar fasciitis, I went to an orthopedic trauma specialist. Later, I had a shamanic session with Eduardo to shine light on any spiritual messages connected to my plantar fasciitis. The Mayan Spirit Guide showed up to tell us he caused it. He explained he didn't mean to create all the physical pain but did want to make sure I remained focused on writing this book.

There was no magical healing after that revelation. But it helped me understand why it happened and made me more committed to avoiding distractions that could keep me from finishing the book.

The spirit world is here to help you. If you will stay open and do your work, it will amaze you at how your life transforms.

Chapter 24

An Overview of
Alternative Healing Options

———— ୬୧୧ ————

There is a wealth of alternative healing choices. The biggest challenge is finding ones that work for you. When I decide to try something new, I first start with research.

- How successful has this type of healing been with other people?

- Can I find any personal recommendations for this healing method or a particular healer?

- Before I schedule an appointment, I like to contact the healer to see how their energy feels to me.

After my first appointment, I check in to evaluate if I want to go back.

- How do my body, mind, and spirit feel?

- Did anything special happen during the healing? New insights? Did any significant healing take place during the session?

- Was there a positive connection between the healer and me?

- If it was an overall positive experience, I give a healer three sessions to decide if this type of healing works for me.

Healers specialize in different areas. Some are fantastic in removing illnesses. Others can help you with emotional, mental, or spiritual issues. Alternative treatments work independently or as a complementary therapy alongside traditional Western medicine. The list below includes the alternative methods I have tried.

Acupuncture: A component of Traditional Chinese Medicine, the practitioner inserts thin needles into the body to clear, activate, and balance a better flow of positive energy.

Acupuncture may relieve symptoms of a variety of problems, including allergies, anxiety, back pain, chemotherapy, dental pain, depression, headaches, hypertension, insomnia, childbirth labor, menstrual cramps, morning sickness, neck pain, osteoarthritis, postoperative nausea and vomiting, respiratory disorders, sprains, and stress.

Check with your doctor if you have a pacemaker, take blood thinners, have a bleeding disorder, or are pregnant.

Affirmations: If we allow negative thoughts, words, and actions to enter our psyche, it can affect our well-being. Affirmations announce our intentions to the Universe, and rewire our brains to be in a more positive state. Write your affirmations and make them part of your daily practice. For example, "I live in a state of abundance, peace, and prosperity." Or, "I am surrounded and filled with Divine light, love, grace, and healing."

You can also buy written affirmation cards to use. When my son was young, affirmations were part of his bedtime routine. Rather than longer sentences, I used affirmation cards with one word. He would pick a card, and then we would discuss what the word meant, why it was important, and what he could do to improve that area of his life.

Affirmative prayer: Focus on positive outcomes, seeing oneself in perfect health.

Aromatherapy: Use incense or an aromatherapy diffuser with essential oils to heighten your sense of smell and contribute to your mood and well-being. If there is a history of asthma, check with your doctor.

Bach flower remedies: Diluted solutions of flowers combined with brandy to make a tincture. You use a dropper to put the tincture under your tongue or in a glass of water. One of the most well-known products is their Rescue Remedy, for stress issues.

Breathwork: Breathing techniques to improve one's mental, emotional, physical, and spiritual states.

Check with your doctor if you take regular medications or if there is a history of cardiovascular issues, glaucoma, panic attacks or psychosis, osteoporosis, recent injuries or surgery, retinal detachment, seizure disorders, mental illness, or antipsychotic medications.

Counting breaths: Dr. Andrew Weil's 4-7-8 breathing technique helps to lower your heart rate, brings you to a more mindful and present state, and can calm you. When overwhelmed, it is a quick way to get some relief. Box breathing incorporates a 4-4-4-4 pattern for a quick boost of mental and physical energy. Coherent breathing uses a 5-5 pattern to increase your sense of calm.

Holotropic breathing: Using sacred music while accelerating your breathing to bring your consciousness to a higher level and access inner healing guidance.

Prana breathing: Also known as pranayama, it is a component of yoga. *Prana* means "life energy," and *yama* means "control." There are various methods and types of controlled pranayama breathing, which can help with stress; improve your sleep quality, lung function, and cognitive performance; lower blood pressure; and reduce cravings.

Rebirthing breathwork: Gentle, shallow breathing to connect with Divine energy. Benefits include a deep state of relaxation, a way to understand and release hidden emotions, heal life trauma, and a deeper connection with the Divine.

Shamanic breathing: During a shamanic drumming journey, you connect and align your breathing with rhythmic drumming, which enhances your journey.

CBD oil and creams: Used for pain relief, anxiety, and depression; to enhance sleep quality; as a complement to cancer treatment to help with nausea, vomiting, and pain; and can help with neurological disorders and high blood pressure.

Additional potential areas CBD oil can help with are schizophrenia and other mental disorders with psychotic symptoms. It can also help change circuits in the brain related to addictions, diabetes, and antitumor qualities.

If you are on medication, ask your doctor before using CBD oil or cream. Check your state and country's law and those of anywhere you travel regarding the legality of using CBD products.

I use CBD oil to improve my sleep. CBD cream was very helpful for plantar fasciitis and reduced the swelling, bruising, and pain I had when I broke a toe.

Chakra energy healing: Chakras are energy points in your body. Energy healing can align and open up blocked chakras, which leads to physical, emotional, mental, and spiritual healing. The main seven chakras are:

Root chakra: This chakra, found at the base of the spine, is about being grounded and safe. If you find yourself worried about money or other survival issues, there's a good chance your root chakra needs work. Red is the color of the root chakra. Stones for the root chakra include black obsidian, tourmaline, bloodstone, mahogany and red coral.

Sacral chakra: A few inches below your belly button, this chakra holds your creative, sexual, and emotional energy. Surround yourself with the color orange if you want to enhance the sacral chakra. Helpful stones for this chakra are tiger's eye, garnet, and orange carnelian.

Solar plexus chakra: This is your power center, your belly, and contributes to your self-esteem, confidence, and self-worth. Wear yellow and work with amber, fire opal, citrine, or topaz if you want to strengthen this chakra.

Heart chakra: You will find your heart chakra in the center of your chest, near your heart. It is associated with love, joy, compassion, and inner peace. The heart chakra connects your physical world to your spiritual world. Green is the color of the heart chakra, and its stones include rose quartz, green agate, green opal, jade and emerald. Pink is the color of the high heart chakra.

Throat chakra: Located at the base of the throat, it affects how you communicate. When it is open and balanced, it will be easier for you to express your authentic self. Add more sky blue colors, and turquoise, aquamarine, kyanite, and blue lace agate help to open, strengthen, and balance this chakra.

Third eye chakra: Found on your forehead, between your eyes, it is important for intuition, imagination, and seeing the big picture. The color indigo and the stones lapis lazuli, sapphire, and sodalite help keep your third eye open and balanced.

Crown chakra: On the top of your head, this chakra represents the spiritual connection with yourself, others, the Universe, and your life purpose. Violet or white are the colors associated with the crown chakra. Use clear quartz, amethyst, or moonstone when you work with the crown.

Chakra sound vibration table: I used to own a BETAR sound vibration chakra table. I loved it! It looks similar to a massage table, with ten speakers underneath the padded area where you lie down. A CD player hooks up to the speakers, allowing you to experience the sound vibrationally all over your body and through the speakers while also listening through a headset.

The BETAR® (Bio-Energetic Transduction-Aided Resonance) design is based on quantum physics. Its sophisticated sound system attunes and aligns you at the highest spiritual level, as it emits frequency patterns at the main chakra energy points. Headphones open the brain and ear to enhanced frequencies of sound. The BETAR speaker system produces a magnetic field of energy that pulses and stimulates your entire nervous system.

Many miracles happened on that table! Besides using the BETAR for myself and my dog, I used it with all my energy healing clients in Asheville and to program my crystals.

Chiropractic: Deals with the diagnosis and treatment of the body's musculoskeletal system. A chiropractor assists with reducing pain and corrects your body's alignment to increase the body's ability to function well.

Chiropractic focuses on bones, cartilage, connective tissue, joints, and muscles. If you suffer from herniated or slipped discs, arthritis, a physical abnormality, or an injury like a fracture, osteoporosis, or fragile health, it is best to first check with your regular doctor.

Craniosacral therapy: Very gentle, light stimulation of the fluids and membranes of your central nervous system. The goal is to relieve tension, eliminate pain, and increase your body's well-being and immune system.

Craniosacral therapy has helped chronic pain, epilepsy, fascia adhesions, fibromyalgia, migraines, multiple sclerosis, neurodegenerative diseases, post-concussion syndrome, speech impairment, stroke, and temporal-mandibular joint syndrome.

Check with your doctor if your history includes an acute stroke, cerebral hemorrhage, aneurysm, cerebral vascular condition with active bleeding, a recent concussion, cerebral swelling, traumatic brain injury, or blood clots.

Crystals: I love working with crystals! They are all over my house, and I also wear them. When I do energy healings, I place crystals on the main chakras of my client's body.

Used for healing and enhanced well-being since the beginning of humankind, there are records of the ancient civilizations of Egypt, Greece, Mexico, China, South America, and New Zealand all using crystals. Considering my memories of past lives in ancient Egypt, Greece, Mexico, and South America, it is not surprising that I resonate with crystals.

Everything on our planet has a unique vibrational frequency. You can choose the type of stone you want to work with depending on what you want to accomplish.

One of my favorite crystal pieces is a necklace with **rose quartz, ruby,** and **blue tourmaline** stones. A longer chain lets it sit right on my heart chakra.

The largest stone is rose quartz, which has the qualities of calmness, compassion, and love. Rose quartz also offers protection, removes negativity, and opens and purifies the heart, promoting an unconditional love of self and others, peace, and a deep level of inner healing.

The next stone is a ruby, which is known for reducing body pain, low energy, heart problems, and helping the body to detox. The ruby is considered a divine creation, enhancing your self-esteem, spiritual wisdom, and intuition.

The last stone is light blue tourmaline, which is known for being the crystal of Spirit. Blue tourmaline increases your happiness, self-confidence, reduces fear, brings more inspiration, tolerance, prosperity, compassion, and balances yin-yang energy. It is a bridge from the physical world to the spiritual realm.

Cupping: Small, heated glass cups are placed on your skin to create a suction. The purpose is to increase your blood flow and the energy in your body. A trained massage therapist, an acupuncturist, or a practitioner of Chinese medicine might offer cupping.

Cupping is used to increase blood flow, relieve pain, and increase relaxation. It can also be beneficial for acne, anxiety, asthma, back pain, bronchitis, cough, diabetes, digestive issues, eczema, fibromyalgia, gout, insomnia, high blood pressure, and shingles.

There have been some reports that cupping can cause scarring or burns if used repeatedly in the same area of the body. I have had massage therapists use cupping on me for multiple concerns and am always happy with the results; I have never experienced issues with cupping.

Check with your doctor if you are pregnant or experience blood clotting problems, bleeding disorders, are menstruating, have fragile skin, recent skin ulcers or wounds, internal organ disorders, a history of strokes, or are on medication.

Diet: A nutritionist, or a holistic or naturopathic doctor can help you find a good diet that can aid in healing. Simple changes in my diet helped me deal with multiple sclerosis. I switched to an anti-inflammatory diet: low fat; low sugar; and no legumes, eggs, soy, gluten, or dairy. The results were amazing. No, it didn't remove the MS, but for the next thirteen years, I remained out of the hospital.

Earthing: Take your shoes off and contact the earth. The electrons from the ground transfer energy into your body, which helps increase your well-being, enhances sleep, blood flow, and lowers inflammation. You also might want to try forest bathing, which originated in Japan as a mindful walk in nature to help with mental or physical healing.

Faith healing: The power of faith and prayer is used to treat mental or physical illnesses or spiritual issues. Typically, faith healers use prayer, healing touch, holy water, and medicinal herbs. Most believe their healing abilities come from God through trance and ecstatic states with the Holy Spirit or ancestral spirits.

Feldenkrais Method: Developed by Moshe Feldenkrais, it is a simple form of movement that improves the body and psychological state and strengthens the connection between the brain and body. Feldenkrais involves somatic sensory-motor learning and brings deeper awareness and connection to one's body through movement.

It's a combination of motor skills, martial arts, psychology, and biomechanics that affects flexibility, coordination, the central nervous system, and assists with cognitive, intention, attention patterns, and healing.

People who practice Feldenkrais report relief of pain, tension, and fatigue; improved concentration and attention; better posture, coordination, and balance; breathing easier; and an increased sense of relaxation and well-being.

Feng shui: Originating in ancient China, feng shui is a way of arranging your surroundings to be in harmony with the natural flow of energy. A bagua is a Chinese feng shui map of eight areas that you want to have in harmony. The bagua areas are family and health, knowledge and wisdom, wealth and prosperity, fame and reputation, helpful people and travel, partnership and marriage, children and creativity, and career and life journey. At the center is the ninth area, which is your overall wellness. Each area has shapes, colors, numbers, seasons, and earth elements that can help balance the energy.

Healing retreat: This is a great way to immerse yourself in various healing modalities. I usually do them in an idyllic setting, like the beach or mountains. Some of my healers and I will conduct online webinars based on the principles of this book. Later, we will also offer in-person healing retreats.

www.ChloeKempWisdomKeeper.com

Herbal medicine: They have used herbs since ancient times for healing and well-being. I recommend you find a holistic nutritionist or natural doctor who can guide you. Check to make sure that you do not interfere with any medication that you may be taking.

Homeopathy: Conceived by a German scientist in 1796, homeopathy believes that the body can cure itself, based on the premise that something that can cause symptoms in the body can also heal the body.

Homeopathic practitioners use diluted substances to treat symptoms of physical and psychological issues. If you are on medication, check with your doctor before starting homeopathic treatment.

Hypnotherapy: Used for treating specific conditions or to change habits. It is a guided process that puts you in a trance state, with the ability to focus your attention and receive suggestions for improving your life.

Infrared sauna: Designed to heat your body, an infrared sauna helps with relaxation, better sleep, improved circulation, pain relief, chronic fatigue syndrome, arthritis, and high blood pressure. If you have psychotic symptoms like hallucinations and delusions, personality disorders, or substance issues, check with your doctor.

Isolation tank: Great for relaxing and meditation. Some also call it a sensory deprivation or float tank. They fill the tank with enough water and Epsom salts for an easy float on your back. With minimal sensory stimulation, it allows you to experience deep meditation. Check with your doctor if you have uncontrolled epilepsy, an infection, open wounds, or serious psychological issues.

Letting go of attachments: One of the basic beliefs in Buddhism is that we suffer because we attach ourselves to certain outcomes. Although it sounds simple, it takes work. You need to not only understand this concept, but also process and consciously use it.

I am much better now, but used to struggle with wanting things to turn out a certain way. There was a point where I completely embraced the concept, and could step back and see the pain and anguish it was causing me to not let go of being attached to a particular outcome. Surrender, trust, and have faith that the Divine is always with you, and knows what is best for you.

Massage therapy: Helps with a range of physical and emotional problems, including reducing pain, anxiety, stress, improving circulation, injuries of the soft tissue, stimulating your lymph system, increasing your range of motion, and heightening your mental alertness.

If you have blood clots, cancer, a contagious disease, fever, inflammation, kidney or liver problems, pregnancy, or uncontrolled hypertension, check with your doctor.

Acupressure massage: Using the principles of acupressure that originated in Japan, it is a deeper form of massage that increases the body's natural energy flow to release tension and balance the body. The concept is very similar to acupuncture, only it doesn't use needles.

Aromatherapy massage: Essential oils are added to the massage oil to increase and enhance the physical and mental well-being benefits of the massage.

Craniosacral therapy massage: Uses light touch to align your central nervous system.

Deep tissue massage: Used for severe muscle tension and pain with musculoskeletal or postural problems or chronic problems. It focuses on the fascia and muscle layers of the body.

Hot stone massage: Hot stones placed on different points of your body are used to go deeper with the massage. The heat from the stones increases your relaxation and helps to loosen up muscle tension.

Lomi lomi massage: A traditional Hawaiian bodywork, also known as the "loving hands massage." The continuous strokes help the body let go of old, ineffective patterns. Lomi means "to knead, to rub, to soothe, to work in and out, as the paws of a contented cat."

It weaves traditional and spiritual concepts with a system of hands-on bodywork to bring harmony and healing to your mind, body, and spirit. This was one of the most loving and nurturing massages I have ever experienced.

Myofascial massage: Used for deeper work on your fascia, the tissue that holds your organs, bones, muscles, and arteries. It helps with restoring your movement and relieving pain.

Reflexology: A technique for stimulating and supporting neural pathways to enhance the functioning and well-being of the body. Firm pressure is applied to certain points in the hands and feet that correlate with other body systems and organs.

Shiatsu: Originating in Japan, it is based on traditional Chinese medicine to work with the qi, the body's natural energy flow, by manipulating the body's natural acupressure points.

Sports massage: Different massage techniques tailored to the athlete and sport to help relieve pain and gain more flexibility and protect from potential injuries.

Swedish massage: Also known as a traditional massage, uses stroking, kneading, and friction to loosen up muscular tension and improve blood circulation. If you are interested in relaxation and relieving muscle tension, this is a good choice.

Thai massage: Combines acupressure, yoga postures, and the principles of Indian Ayurvedic traditions to work on your entire body. Besides your massage therapist using their palms and fingers to apply firm pressure, they will also stretch your body and place you in unique positions while guiding you with breathwork. People have experienced pain relief, better posture, and an increased body range of motion.

Therapeutic massage: A more gentle massage includes applying pressure, holding, and moving your muscles, ligaments, tendons, and fascia.

Medical intuitive: Intuitive guidance is used to determine the causes of physical or emotional problems. While most don't make a formal diagnosis, many medical intuitives work with doctors to provide second opinions. It works as a complementary form of alternative healing to find the root cause of a problem.

Moxibustion: Mugwort root is burned and placed near the body to help with healing by warming and energizing the blood, stimulating the qi (vital energy flow), strengthening the kidneys, and removing stagnation.

Naturopathy: Health care that includes alternative, natural, and modern medical therapies. The primary principles include aiding the body to self-heal, resolving underlying issues by making a holistic treatment plan that incorporates the body, mind, and spirit, and focusing on education and prevention.

Some conditions naturopathy can help include ADHD, allergies, anxiety, stress, depression, autoimmune conditions, autism, cancer, diabetes, digestive problems, cardiovascular problems, headaches, hormonal imbalance, infections, menopause, neurodegenerative conditions, obesity, respiratory conditions, skin conditions, and stress.

Nutritional supplements: Your doctor or nutritionist can help you choose which supplements to take. My young internist learned that low vitamin D levels can affect multiple sclerosis. My vitamin D levels were so low, I had to take a prescription-strength dose to get it to an acceptable level. I take 4,000 IU of vitamin D to keep my levels healthy. Blood work is very helpful to determine if your body has low levels of vitamins, minerals, or hormones.

Past life regression: Many times, trauma from a past life can still affect you in your current life. A licensed past life therapist uses guided hypnosis to help you look at your past. The International Board for Regression Therapy (IBRT) licensed John Williams, the regression therapist I use in Asheville. An appointment for a comprehensive past life regression lasts around two hours.

Pilates: Used as an alternative for rehabilitation therapy, Pilates is low impact. Influenced by yoga, ballet and calisthenics, it promotes better flexibility, balance, body awareness, and strength.

Check with your doctor before starting an intense Pilates practice if you are pregnant, over forty, have musculoskeletal problems, are out of shape, have had recent surgery, or other serious medical problems.

Psychic healing: Somewhat similar to a medical intuitive, a psychic healer can assist you in understanding your illness and tap into spirit messages about how to heal it. I have had an amazing relationship with a psychic healer for thirteen years. When dealing with significant healing issues, he has always been on point.

Qigong: An element of traditional Chinese medicine, qigong uses meditation, movement, and breathwork to enhance your vital energy. It also can improve immunity and blood circulation, relieve stress and anxiety, and improve flexibility, balance, and focus.

Similar to acupuncture, qigong activates meridians, organs, and acupuncture points in the body. If you have a history of psychotic disorders, check with your doctor.

Reflexology: Some massage therapists will incorporate reflexology into your massage. Or, you can find a reflexologist to give you a session. It is based on the theory that areas in the foot and hands correspond to organs in the body. You can also buy hand and foot reflexology charts to work on yourself.

Reflexology can be beneficial for anxiety and stress, and to relieve emotional and physical pain. It also works well as a complementary treatment for illnesses like cancer.

Check with your doctor before getting reflexology if you are pregnant, have an active infection, arthritis in your foot or ankle, circulation problems, certain types of cancer, diabetes, foot fractures, kidney stones, gallstones, kidney stones, or an open wound.

Rolfing: A method for changing and improving the body to provide long-lasting relief. This deep-tissue bodywork focuses on restructuring muscles and fascia. It can help with posture and chronic muscular-skeletal pain and conditions. If there are circulatory problems, cardiopulmonary or musculoskeletal disease, neurological disorders, or high stress levels, check with your doctor.

Salt cave therapy (heliotherapy): In a salt cave, you breathe in negatively charged ions. This can help reduce inflammation and mucus and problems with respiratory conditions like sinus congestion, bronchitis, asthma, or COPD.

Check with your doctor if you have active infections, blood disorders, fever, cardiovascular problems, high blood pressure, hyperthyroidism, malignant diseases, open wounds, respiratory failure, or tuberculosis.

Shamanism: An ancient spiritual practice that is found all over the world. My shamanic experiences have been with Indigenous shamans from Ecuador, Peru, and Mexico. In an ecstatic trance state, a shaman connects with the spirit world to heal physical, mental, emotional, and spiritual problems. Shamans master the ability to move between altered states at will.

Besides healing, shamans may perform ceremonies, create art, chant, sing, play instruments, trance dance, forecast future events, communicate with the spirit world, and help souls return to the Light. Aligned with nature, shamans can communicate with plants, animals, the elements, and the spirit world.

A shamanic healing session may include sound, herbs, plants, rattles and drums, feathers, crystals, essential oils, bodywork, eggs, candles, incense, or a limpia (a spiritual cleansing using herbs and prayers to clear and balance the mind, body, and spirit of negative energy, entities or thoughts).

They may also perform a soul retrieval. When a person experiences trauma, part of your being may splinter, flee, or hide, which shamans call soul loss. The shaman does healing work to restore and bring the missing part of your soul back into your life.

Sound healing therapy: Sound can strengthen your entire well-being. It has helped people with anxiety, autism, behavioral and psychiatric disorders, cancer, dementia, and depression. People report reducing the risk of cardiovascular disease and stroke, lowering blood pressure and cholesterol, sleep improvement, and stabilizing mood swings. Sound has been instrumental in my spiritual awakening and healing work.

Sound immersion healing: A specialty of River Guerguerian, he plays percussion instruments on and over your body while you are lying down in a meditative state. I have had extraordinary experiences with River's sound immersions.

Voice sound healing: A person uses their voice to emit sounds and tones for healing.

Other sound healing methods: Includes chanting, praying out loud, humming, singing, listening to music, dancing, meditating to sound, tuning forks, or playing an instrument. When having surgery, bring headphones and a curated list of healing music to listen to while you are in surgery and recovery.

Tai chi: A type of Chinese martial arts that offers health benefits, meditation, and defense training. It can improve flexibility and balance; increase energy, stamina, and muscle strength; and reduce anxiety and stress.

Tai chi may also improve symptoms of congestive heart failure, joint pain, lower blood pressure, strengthen your immunity, and reduce risks of falling. It is a gentle and graceful low-impact form of exercise. If you have back pain, fractures, a hernia, joint problems, severe osteoporosis, or are pregnant, consult with your doctor.

Tapping (Emotional Freedom Technique – EFT): Also referred to as psychological acupressure, tapping balances your energy and helps with physical and emotional pain. Like acupuncture, it focuses on your body's meridian points. Instead of acupuncture needles, tapping fingertips are used to apply pressure to the energy points while focusing on one problem at a time.

EFT helps with pain relief, insomnia, anxiety, depression, and post-traumatic stress disorder (PTSD). If you have an obsessive-compulsive disorder, check with your doctor.

Traditional Chinese Medicine (TCM): Over two thousand years old, TCM includes acupuncture, acupressure, cupping or scraping, dietary therapy, exercise (qigong, tai chi), herbal medicine, massage, meditation, and moxibustion.

TCM can help with allergies, anxiety, arthritis, diabetes, fertility issues, high blood pressure, insomnia, menopause, obesity, pain, Parkinson's disease, and skin conditions. If you are pregnant or nursing, scheduled for upcoming surgery, on medication, are elderly, or are seeking treatment for a child, consult with your doctor.

Transpersonal therapy: A holistic mind-body approach to talk therapy, which incorporates an individual's physical, mental, emotional, social, creative, and spiritual healing needs. It combines Western and Eastern philosophy, mysticism, and cognitive psychology with meditation, visualization, and hypnotherapy. For me, it is a quick and powerful process that often can uncover the core issue and resolution of a situation, many times in only one session.

Visualization: Using your mind to visualize or imagine a healthy, happy, and relaxed body and mind. Also called guided imagery or creative visualization, one focuses attention on what you would like to occur in your life. Visualization therapy can change your emotional patterns, bringing positive physical changes.

Many use visualization techniques for anxiety, asthma, enhanced mental or physical performance, fibromyalgia, insomnia, stopping smoking, and weight loss. You can do it on your own or in a group; in the beginning, it will be easier to use guided instructions and imagery.

Yoga: A body and mind practice developed in India over five thousand years ago, includes breathing techniques, meditation, movement, and relaxation.

Yoga can help with arthritis, cardiovascular problems, and pain. It also improves sleep quality, flexibility, balance, and strength; increases your physical and mental energy; stabilizes your mood; and helps you manage stress and anxiety better.

Consult with your doctor if you have a risk of blood clots, diabetes, eye conditions like glaucoma, a herniated disk, cardiovascular problems, severe balance issues, or osteoporosis. Tell your yoga instructor if you are pregnant.

Hatha yoga — Good for stress management. It has a slower pace and easier poses and movements.

Vinyasa yoga – A series of yoga poses that flow into one another.

Ashtanga yoga – A flow class that links your breathing to the movement and poses.

Iyengar yoga – Uses straps, blocks, and chairs to help move and align the body.

Yin yoga — A meditative, slow-paced class with seated postures.

Restorative yoga — Used for relaxation and meditation.

Anusara yoga – A more modern version of hatha yoga that focuses on mind-body-heart connection.

Yoga nidra – Full-body guided meditation for relaxation and sleep.

Hot yoga – Practiced in a room heated to high temperatures while doing a series of twenty-six challenging poses.

Power yoga — High-intensity class that focuses on building muscle.

Kundalini yoga – Focuses on releasing the kundalini energy coiled in the lower spine. Classes may also include meditation, mantras, and chanting.

Jivamukti yoga — Similar to vinyasa, it also has a component of Hindu spiritual principles.

Prenatal yoga – Uses props and safe movements to increase your stability.

Acro yoga – Done with a partner or group, it combines acrobatics with yoga.

Aerial yoga – Instead of a yoga mat, you use a silk hammock suspended from the ceiling to support you while doing the poses.

Chapter 25

Healing Is an Ongoing Process

———— ༈༈༈ ————

S piritual healing is not a one-time event. Spirit will let you know when it is time to do more work.

When I started writing this book, my Mexican shaman told me I was beginning a powerful personal transformation. Since then, there have been periods where I was aware I was burning off victim energy. In this lifetime and other past lives, many things happened to me that caused me to suffer.

How much stress can you handle before you become overwhelmed? If only a few difficult things happen close together, I am fine. Recently, I had seven significant things happen, all within a twenty-four-hour period, which was way over my limit to handle well. With all the negative third dimension things that occurred, I felt bombarded, and allowed it to get me stuck with feelings of overwhelm.

Surrounded by heaviness and a dark mood, I took my dog for a walk. We went to the mountain near my house; I needed to be in the forest, communing with nature. Meditating and talking with my Spirit Guides was comforting. Tears rolled down my cheeks when I realized the recent experiences of this week were bumping up against old wounds.

I knew I needed to talk with Eduardo. I loved his response.

"Chloe, I understand these recent events have been challenging for you. But, it is a good thing. You are integrating everything you learned and remembered while writing your book. Although it can be painful, it is a necessary step."

I told him I thought the deeper grief I was experiencing was about the trauma that happened when I was three.

"Chloe, your deep grief is not only about this lifetime. You are also clearing all your past life trauma."

That made sense to me. I need to shed all the parts of all of my lives that no longer serve my highest purpose.

The next morning, I woke up clearer, stronger, lighter, and more peaceful. Everything that had happened this week was to get my attention that it is time to burn up more victim energy. The first message I received was, "You are not a victim anymore."

Answers and solutions to things I had been struggling with started coming to me with ease. I stepped out of my victim body into a new higher plane, refreshed and ready to tackle whatever Spirit wants me to do.

To help me with the integration, I wrote several affirmations. For me, visual reminders are an effective way for me to embody my lessons. Usually, I write affirmations in a positive format. This time, I wanted to send a powerful message to myself about what I will no longer tolerate.

- What do I need to do to be in integrity with myself?

First, define what "integrity" means to you. Next, visualize how that can show up in your life. Determine how you want to be treated by others. Who fills you up? Which people drain your energy? Are you spending your time wisely? Have you been neglecting your self-care? Are you satisfied and content with your relationships?

- I do not need other people's opinions or permission to do what is best for me.

You can't be in integrity with others until you are in integrity with yourself. No one has to agree or approve of your personal choices. As you learn to trust your spiritual guidance, there will be less need to seek input from others. Hold the intention that your thoughts, actions, and feelings will come from a place of love and compassion, not just for others, but for yourself.

- I don't allow people to persuade me that my truth is false, or try to shame me for my thoughts and feelings.

Not everyone wants to accept the new you—the one who stands in your power and integrity. Some people will try to convince you that you're on the wrong track. Many times, that attitude comes from their own fear of change. Your staying the same is comforting to them, but you pay the price. When you do things you know in your heart are not good for you, it creates unnecessary problems in your life.

- I only allow people in my inner circle who are in alignment with my highest good and respect my sacred, authentic self.

For me, this one has been challenging. Where do you draw the line? Wanting to be compassionate with others, many times I allowed myself to fall into the trap of slowly letting my boundaries move to an unhealthy place. Do you hang on to relationships, way beyond their expiration date, because it is easier than taking action? For the past several years, I have been rearranging who belongs in my inner circle—who will remain as a casual friend and who I will remove from my third dimension life. I am no longer willing to ignore my integrity and needs.

- My intuition guides and protects me in all my relationships. I accept and honor the sacred truth of my relationships.

Not everyone will honor your boundaries. Before I move someone from my inner circle, first I try discussing with them how I would like to see the relationship strengthen. If they are open to an honest and nonjudgmental discussion, hopefully you can come to a mutual understanding and agreement of how your relationship will go forward. However, you risk losing them if they are not willing to accept your boundaries.

Even though you decided it was unhealthy to continue the relationship without some changes, you might experience a sense of loss if they dissolve the relationship. It is a little like breaking up with a partner—you imagined this person would always be in your life. But, you know deep in your heart, your highest good is not in alignment with them.

Yet, you dread having to decide to pull the plug. Here is where your boundaries come into play. You must decide what you can live with now. The situation may change in the future, but all we truly have is the present. In your life today, what is best for your highest good? Does the negativity of having this person in your life outweigh the benefits?

- I banish all confusion about what is real in my relationships with others.

Your sacred truth comes from within. Don't allow other people to confuse you. Spirit will always point you toward what is best for you. Trust your inner guidance; it is real.

- I no longer engage with anyone who tries to gaslight me.

The Miriam Webster dictionary defines gaslighting as, "The psychological manipulation of a person, usually over an extended period, that causes the victim to question the validity of their own thoughts, perception of reality, or memories and typically leads to confusion, loss of confidence and self-esteem, uncertainty of one's emotional or mental stability, and a dependency on the perpetrator."

In my recent deep sadness, I shed many tears for how often I allowed myself to be manipulated by family, friends, and partners. Rather than admitting and taking responsibility for their actions, they would twist the truth to put the blame on anyone but themselves. Or they would insist things had not happened. Over time, I felt worn down. I second-guessed myself, and found it difficult to make decisions or trust my truth. Gaslighting keeps you in a perpetual state of confusion.

- I am not obligated to sacrifice my peace, serenity and truth to placate others.

How long will you let unhealthy situations continue? One of my problems in this lifetime has been giving people too many chances. As a young child, I wanted to believe I could count on my family. What I got in return was a continuous stream of broken promises. Even with family, you can reach a point where you are no longer willing to accept that type of behavior.

- I always honor and respect my truth.

No more doubts or second-guessing. No longer will I allow myself to compromise my truth in my relationships with others.

- I release all victim thoughts, feelings, and energy from my mind, body, spirit and space; in all ways, at all times, in all realities and all dimensions.

When Eduardo told me I was grieving for every lifetime that I didn't honor my truth, it resonated with me. It is time to let go of all the negativity I experienced in my many lives here on Earth. I want to more completely own and step into my authentic, sacred life.

No more wishing or hoping that things will change. This time, I am committed to do whatever it takes to release and let go of everything that is not serving my highest purpose.

Increase your self-care

When you are experiencing extra stress, it is a good idea to increase your self-care. My intuition guided me to add some extra self-nurturing to help me stay grounded and centered during this healing process.

- ❤ Homeopathic supplement to help with stress.
- ❤ New aromatherapy product to improve the quality of my sleep.
- ❤ Spend more time in the forest.
- ❤ Add healing crystal bowls and chimes music to my daily listening.
- ❤ Buy another wind chime for one of the outdoor areas of my house.
- ❤ A commitment to not rehash the negative things that have happened.
- ❤ Let go of attachments to outcomes. As I remain committed to being my best self, I trust Spirit knows what is best for me. I will live the life Spirit has planned for me.
- ❤ To enhance my coping skills of isolating during the pandemic, I bought a beautiful lounging outfit. Since I am spending a great deal of time by myself, I decided I deserve something nice to wear. It will bring me joy and remind me I am worth it; I don't need a special occasion or need to wear it for anyone other than myself. I Am Enough ❤

Does this mean once I master this healing, I will not experience any more problems?

No. Similar to peeling an onion, we all have multiple layers of experiences in our current and past lives. When the spirit world thinks you are ready, they will give you the opportunity to clear and heal more wounds.

Digging deep is hard work. It asks you to address buried and forgotten issues. Spirit encourages you to bring them to the Light, so that you can learn everything those experiences came to teach you. Although it can be challenging, the reward is worth it.

Shut your eyes for a few minutes. Take a few deep breaths. Visualize yourself free from the bonds that hold you back from becoming your authentic self. Breath in the ease and grace you will experience in your life as you continue your healing spiritual journey. Remember, as you heal yourself and raise your vibration, you are also helping to heal the world.

Chapter 26

How You Can Help Heal the World

━━━━━⟋⟋⟍⟍━━━━━

One of the best things you can do is heal yourself and connect to your spirituality. As you increase your emotional, mental, physical, and spiritual well-being, your vibrational energy will rise. When you connect to Spirit, it helps raise the vibration of the entire planet. The sooner you accept we are all in this together—we are all one—the better it will be for the world.

Focus on what connects us rather than what divides us

We are in a crisis of division. There is fighting about everything—politics, the economy, health, equality, social responsibility, people's rights, history, climate change, how to deal with the pandemic. It is easy to fall into an "us against them" mentality.

I am inviting you to step back and find what you have in common with people who hold very different views from you. Look at them, gaze into their eyes, try connecting to their souls. They are somebody's child, parent, brother, or sister. Attempt to find a connection. Choose to find at least one thing you like about the person. They don't have to become your best friend. All I am asking you to do is see them with fresh eyes and an open attitude.

Look for common ground to help ease the tension and communicate without creating more conflict. Be in the moment, to hold space for you and this person to see each other differently. If it feels too difficult to hold neutral space, you can always cut the encounter short. Remind yourself they are doing the best they can with what they know. You don't have to agree or like what they do. If we see everyone as our brothers and sisters, it is more difficult to see them as our staunch enemy.

Does that mean you need to abandon your beliefs to fit in with others? No! I want you to be your authentic self. You can always limit topics for discussion with certain people. I think it will surprise you that the more you share your authentic sacred self with others, the more compassion and understanding will grow between you. Your willingness to share your truth encourages them to do the same.

Recently I saw an acquaintance. We are on the opposite spectrum of many topics. Since I am working on sharing all of my authentic truth, I am not interested in trying to censor myself. I watched his reaction when I mentioned I work with a shaman. Sensing that he accepted that this was my path, there was no need for him to decide if he would ever go to a shaman or to think differently of me because I do.

Over time, we established a genuine connection by finding and nourishing what we have in common. You don't have to be a mirror image of another person's beliefs. We appreciate our commonalities and don't exert pressure to conform to each other's beliefs.

Everyone desires to be seen, heard, and understood. If we want others to accept who we are, don't we need to do the same? I am not saying to accept the actions of someone who is causing harm to others or our planet. A shift in your attitude can make a significant change. Send love to everyone. You can't control how they receive, view, or accept you. But you can control your actions. Be on the side of love. Be an example of how to treat others.

I recently found some incorrect charges on a bill, and I had to call customer service, one of my least favorite things. I find it is better to wait until I am not tired or hungry to make those calls. This was the third time I had called to straighten out the problem.

Rather than trying to rush me through, she stopped and listened to me. Her communication skills were outstanding! The tone and words she used were perfect. She said she agreed that this should not have required three calls to fix. Then she took care of the problem that the other two representatives could not do.

I felt surrounded by Divine light. My anger and frustration melted away. This call could have gone differently if she had treated me like the "enemy" and not listened to me. She talked with me, rather than at me.

The act of hearing, seeing, and acknowledging another person is a powerful gift. Imagine if you were trying to discuss global warming with a nonbeliever. What if first you asked them why they have certain beliefs about global warming? Then, instead of arguing, repeat what they said to show them you heard it correctly. Gaze into their eyes, sending loving-kindness to their heart. Now take a few deep breaths, and share some of your global warming beliefs with them. If we can avoid the "I'm right, you are wrong" energy, it will enhance your communication with others.

The Buddhist Loving Kindness meditation blessing can help you with this practice. There are many versions of the Loving Kindness meditation. You can use one below or customize your own.

Sit with your eyes closed. Take some deep breaths. Clear your mind.

First, you begin with yourself:

"May I be happy."

"May I be safe."

"May I be healthy, peaceful, and strong."

"May I give and receive appreciation today."

Now repeat the blessing for all sentient beings:

"May you be happy."

"May you be safe."

"May you be healthy, peaceful, and strong."

"May you give and receive appreciation today."

—*VeryWellMind.com,*
"How to Practice Loving Kindness Meditation"

<u>*Other examples of the Loving Kindness blessing:*</u>

"May I be filled with loving-kindness."

"May I be well in body and mind."

"May I be at ease and happy."

"May you be filled with loving-kindness."

"May you be well in body and mind."

"May you be at ease and happy."

—JackKornfield.com
Meditation on Loving Kindness

Think about it for a second. If your enemies have plenty of loving-kindness, safety, wellness, and happiness, they have a better chance of having a more open and compassionate mind. Who knows, they may even think about awakening and enlightenment. We don't always know how we affect others. At the very least, you showed them how to be empathic, kind, and compassionate, even when you don't agree with each other.

You will also witness changes in your own life. When you come from a place of loving-kindness, it fills your life with more compassion and empathy. When you are in that space, it is easier for others to hear and accept what you are saying.

Based on my spiritual experiences and information from my Spirit Guides, nothing will produce lasting change unless more people wake up to their spiritual purpose. We are out of balance with our world. Many things that are happening right now are trying to get our attention, wake us up, and get us to think and act differently.

How do we find balance?

When you get your spiritual life in order, everything else falls into place. You go from a more ego-centered place of making something happen to trusting that you will be guided at the right time to take action. Yes, you still need to take action. We are in human bodies; we are the ones on this planet who need to do the legwork to help heal the world.

Resist the urge to take on too many things at once. If you spread yourself too thin, you are more apt to become burned out. Start with one cause. Determine how you can best be of service. Find out what is being done. Do you want to be one of the "boots on the ground" people, or are you more of a "behind-the-scenes" person? What skills do you offer?

Once you have chosen the causes you want to support, please do your best to do your work with compassion, empathy, and love. Do you remember the saying, "You can catch more flies with honey than vinegar?" It is a simple reminder that we respond better when someone treats us kindly rather than treating us as the enemy.

When I was writing the chapter about the Star Children, I started receiving visions about a Millennial Movement. As I mentioned, not all millennials, Generation Z, and Alphas came in as Star Children. You don't have to be a Star Child to help heal the world. However, as they remember who they are, and what their purpose is, it will be the Star Children who will have the biggest impact.

I envision Millennial Movement events all over the world. Besides sharing spiritual information, it will be an opportunity for people to connect in a bigger way with causes that are important to them. You can sign up to help, globally or locally.

The Millennial Movement is for all people and of all ages. It's time to create a true multigenerational approach for healing the world. We all bring skills and talents. I would love to see musicians, actors, tech experts, and other powerful people join to help heal the world.

What action will you take to help heal the world?

Do you want to be an individual healer?

Have you had any experience with healing others?

Which type of healing interests you more?

- Spiritual
- Physical
- Emotional
- Mental

Are you willing to receive training to become a healer?

Which healing methods resonate the most with you?

Are you in the creative arts?

Many times, Spirit talks to us through the arts.

Music, lyrics, visual arts, the spoken and written word can bring powerful messages and affect our mood.

Which causes do you resonate with the most?

- Addiction
- Animal rights

- Deforestation
- Discrimination
- Dismantle white supremacy
- Economic problems
- Education
- Environment
- Equality for everyone
- Food insecurity
- Food shortages
- Gender rights
- Global warming and climate change
- Hatred
- Health care
- Homelessness
- Human trafficking
- Income equality
- Inclusivity
- Isolation and loneliness
- Mental health
- Migration and immigration
- Nature protection and preservation
- Pandemics
- Police brutality
- Pollution

- Poverty
- Racism
- Reparations
- Surveillance
- Sustainable consumerism
- Water shortages
- Women's rights
- Violence

Yes, the world has many significant problems. Many of the causes overlap. This list is to help you find which areas you are most drawn to help. Add to the list.

Broaden your views and horizons

When something isn't creating problems in our immediate environment, it is easy to become complacent. We can fall into the "us/them" mentality without realizing it. Just because something is not happening in your backyard doesn't mean it isn't a problem or that you don't need to help.

This is where your spiritual growth can help. As you continue on your awakening path, you see the world differently. You experience the interconnectedness of everyone and everything. When you live in an empathic and compassionate place, you can no longer turn a blind eye to others' plights.

That's where making a list of priorities you want to tackle comes into play. We as individuals don't have the energy or resources to fight everything all at once. So, narrow down your support to your top choices. Then make your plan and do something. It's too easy to convince yourself that you are just one person—how can you make a real difference? If we all had that attitude, nothing would get done. Trust that the right people will show up at the right time to help. Your actions can be the inspiration others need to become involved.

Sometimes a simple act can make a significant difference over time

Be mindful of your thoughts and deeds. Create new habits. Start by choosing a cause that you can support. Commit to taking action; implement ways to hold yourself accountable.

Or, how about creating a challenge? Ask your family and friends to join you in healing the world. Encourage and hold each other accountable. Take turns choosing the next set of actions you will all take.

I found an interesting piece, "101 Ways to Heal the Earth," originally published in 1989 in Global Climate Change by the Context Institute. I included this piece to show we have been aware for decades that we need to do our part to slow down climate change. Sadly, we did not do enough and are now facing the serious consequences of our inaction.

I hope you are already aware of most of the things on the list. Read it anyway. It is time we were all reminded about what we can do. When this list was first created, I imagine the mainstream population did not accept many things as necessary. Thirty years later, we have much bigger climate problems that require much bigger solutions.

"101 Ways to Heal the Earth"

What can one person do to avert climate change? The answer is a lot. This list of 101 suggestions doesn't begin to exhaust the possibilities; use it as a creative jumping-off point and come up with your own ways to make an impact.

The unifying themes here are changes in lifestyle that: (1) reduce energy usage and slow down the fires of industrialism; (2) protect and restore the environment so that its climate-stabilizing mechanisms are preserved; (3) increase individual participation in government and economic decisions; and (4) facilitate a deep personal commitment to caring for the Earth.

The point is not to feel guilty for not doing all 101, but to use this list to empower yourself and your friends to take action. Find one thing you can do, do it, and then find another. By such incremental steps are long journeys made.

The list is distilled from three sources: "The Greenhouse Crisis: 101 Ways to Save the Earth," published by the Greenhouse Crisis Foundation; "Personal Action Guide for the Earth," published by the Transmissions Project for the UN Environment Programme; and Context Institute research.

1. Insulate your home.
2. Buy energy-efficient appliances.
3. Caulk and weatherstrip doors and windows.
4. Install storm windows.
5. Close off unused areas in your home from heat and air conditioning.
6. Wear warm clothing and turn down winter heat.

7. Switch to low-wattage or fluorescent light bulbs.

8. Turn off all lights that don't need to be on.

9. Use cold water instead of hot whenever possible.

10. Opt for small-oven or stove-top cooking when preparing small meals.

11. Run dishwashers only when full.

12. Set refrigerators to 38 degrees Fahrenheit and the freezer to 5 degrees Fahrenheit.

13. Run clothes washers full, but don't overload them.

14. Use moderate amounts of biodegradable detergent.

15. Air-dry your laundry when possible.

16. Clean the lint screen in the clothes dryer.

17. Instead of ironing, hang clothes in the bathroom while showering.

18. Take quick showers instead of baths.

19. Install water-efficient shower heads and sink-faucet aerators.

20. Install air-assisted or composting toilets.

21. Collect rainwater and greywater for gardening use.

22. Insulate your water heater. Turn it down to 121 Fahrenheit.

23. Plant deciduous shade trees that protect windows from summer sun but allow it in during the winter.

24. Explore getting a solar water heater for your home.

25. Learn how to recycle all your household goods, from clothing to motor oil to appliances.

26. Start separating your newspaper, other paper, glass, aluminum, and food wastes.

27. Encourage your local recycling center or program to accept plastic.

28. Urge local officials to begin roadside pickup of recyclables and hazardous waste.

29. Encourage friends, neighbors, businesses, local organizations to recycle and sponsor recycling efforts.

30. Use recycled products, especially paper.

31. Reuse envelopes, jars, paper bags, scrap paper, etc.

32. Bring your canvas bags to the grocery store.

33. Encourage local governments to buy recycled paper.

34. Start a recycling program where you work.

35. Limit or eliminate your use of "disposable" items.

36. Urge fast-food chains to use recyclable packaging.

37. Avoid using anything made of plastic foam. They often make it from CPCs, and it is never biodegradable.

38. If your car gets less than 35 mpg, sell it; buy a small fuel-efficient model and spend whatever money you save on home energy efficiency.

39. Maintain and tune up your vehicle regularly for maximum gas mileage.

40. Join a carpool or use public transport to commute.

41. Write to automobile manufacturers to let them know you intend to buy the most fuel-efficient car on the road.

42. Reduce your air-conditioning.

43. Encourage auto centers to install CFC recycling equipment for auto air conditioners. They release Freon during servicing to become both greenhouse gas and an ozone layer destroyer.

44. Remove unnecessary articles from your car. Every hundred pounds of weight decreases fuel efficiency by one percent.

45. Don't speed.

46. Walk or use a bicycle whenever possible.

47. Urge the local government to enact restrictions on automobile use in congested areas downtown.

48. Enjoy sports and recreational activities that use your muscles rather than gasoline and electricity.

49. Buy products that will last.

50. Rent or borrow items you don't use often.

51. Maintain and repair the items you own.

52. Use colored fabrics to avoid the need for bleach.

53. Use natural fiber clothing, bedding, and towels.

54. Don't buy aerosols, halo fire extinguishers, or other products containing CFCs.

55. Write to computer chip manufacturers and urge them to stop using CFC-113 as a solvent.

56. Invest your money in environmentally and socially conscious businesses.

57. Avoid rainforest products and inform the supplier or manufacturer of your concerns.

58. Use postcards instead of letters for brief messages.

59. Eat vegetarian foods as much as possible. Meat makes less efficient use of land, soil, water, and energy—and cows emit 300 liters of methane per day.

60. Buy locally produced foods; avoid buying foods that must be trucked in from great distances.

61. Read labels. Eat organic or less-processed foods.

62. Start a garden; plant a garden instead of a lawn.

63. Water the garden with an underground drip system.

64. Support organic farming and gardening methods; shun chemical fertilizers, herbicides, and pesticides.

65. Compost kitchen and garden waste, or give it to a friend who can.

66. Inform schools, hospitals, airlines, restaurants, and the media of your concerns.

67. Stay informed about the state of the Earth.

68. Talk to friends, relatives, and co-workers about preventing global climate change.

69. Read and support publications that educate about long-term sustainability.

70. Start a global climate change study group.

71. Educate children about sustainable living practices.

72. Copy this list and give it to ten friends.

73. Go on a citizen diplomacy trip and talk with those you meet about averting global climate change.

74. Get involved in local tree-planting programs.

75. Join an environmental organization. If they're not involved with climate change, get them involved.

76. Support zero population growth.

77. Support work to alleviate poverty. Poverty causes deforestation and other environmental problems.

78. Donate money to environmental organizations.

79. Support programs that aim to save rainforest areas.

80. Support solar and renewable energy development.

81. Work to protect local watershed areas.

82. Pave as little as possible. Rip up excess concrete.

83. Encourage sewage plants to compost their sludge.

84. Write your senator now to support S. 201, the World Environment Policy Act.

85. Write your congressperson now to support H.R. 1078, the Global Warming Prevention Act.

86. Support disarmament and the redirection of military funds to environmental restoration.

87. Write letters to the editor expressing your concerns about climate change and environmental issues.

88. Support electoral candidates who run on environmental platforms.

89. Run for local office on an environmental platform.

90. Attend city council meetings and speak out for action on climate change issues.

91. Organize a citizen's initiative to put a local "climate protection program" into place.

92. Learn how to lobby. Lobby your local, state, and national elected officials for action on climate change and environmental issues.

93. Organize a demonstration at a plant that uses CFCs.

94. In place of TV and the stereo, spend time reading, writing, drawing, telling stories, and making music.

95. Live within the local climate as much as possible, rather than trying to isolate yourself from it.

96. Strive to establish good communication with friends, neighbors, and family, including learning conflict resolution skills.

97. Spend time seeing, hearing, and rejoicing in the beauty of the Earth. Feel your love for the Earth. Make serving the Earth your first priority.

98. Learn about the simplistic, less resource-intensive lifestyles of aboriginal peoples.

99. Think often about the kind of Earth you would like to see for your grandchildren's grandchildren.

100. While doing small things, think big. Think about redesigning cities, restructuring the economy, re-conceiving humanity's role on the Earth.

101. Pray, visualize, hope, meditate, dream.

This list is a good example of how individual action can make a difference. Make your to-do list for the causes you choose to support. Be mindful of your actions. It is no longer enough to have the intention of helping heal our world. You must put your beliefs and priorities into action. We are running out of time.

A significant part of healing the world is to awaken your spiritual life's purpose. Pray and meditate for guidance and understanding of your specific role in helping our planet. We all have important roles to play.

If I have accomplished nothing else with this book, I pray I have inspired and motivated you to embrace your spiritual side. If we don't increase our spiritual awareness, all the other things we might do to heal the world won't make a lasting difference. My visions and my Spirit Guides have made it clear that the many problems our planet is facing are symptoms of being out of balance with ourselves and the world. Mother Earth is showing us she will no longer go down this path.

The problems are here to get our attention, to wake us up. Make that your priority. Although we are running out of time, we can still create a different outcome.

Do not become complacent. Do not wait for others to rescue the world. Step up and do your part now.

Chapter 27

The Rescue Team Arrives

In 2011, I had an amazing prophetic dream. I had been struggling with frustration about my Spirit Guides telling me they would not intervene to relieve all the tragedy and suffering on Earth until more people woke up. I think my guides wanted to give me hope that help will come.

It was one of the most profound dreams I have ever experienced. More than just a lucid dream, I felt like I was there, as if I had traveled to the future. Everything was so real and vivid. My intuition told me to protect this dream by not revealing the details to anyone. The most I ever mentioned was that they will rescue us when enough people awaken to their spiritual purpose.

I kept the dream to myself since I was concerned that people might try to block the rescue mission. Although I trusted her, I didn't even share the dream details with my dream interpreter. I was receiving spirit messages to not talk about the dream on the Internet, and we were doing all our work online.

When I moved to Oaxaca City in January 2020, I met a U.S. college professor doing research for her academic book about shamanism in Mexico. She asked to interview me. I thought she only wanted me to tell her about my experience working with shamans. She also wanted to learn about my own shamanic abilities. After a couple of hours into her interview, I felt a sense of trust and told her about the rescue dream. But it was strictly off-record.

So, why am I willing to share the dream now in this book? It feels like we are at a tipping point. I have reached a point of clarity that it is the right time to share everything. When I am at peace and no longer have concerns about sharing the dream, that is my sign that it is time to move forward. It is all about trust.

Like the prophecy about the Spiritual Grandmothers being asked to share their most sacred secrets, I am letting go of protecting this sacred secret dream and trusting that whoever needs to know about the rescue will find it here. My intentions with everything I have put in this book are to help more people wake up.

Welcome to the future

The dream began with me and my sister unpacking the trunk of her car after a trip.

My phone rings.

"Hello."

"This is your father."

"How can that be possible? You have been dead for decades."

My father answered, "Look up."

"What? Why are you asking me to look up?"

He replied, "The Pink Ones are here."

I glanced up at the sky, stunned that little pink tulle-like parachutes covered the entire sky.

"I don't understand. There are little pink parachutes everywhere, but I don't see any people."

My dad responded, "That's because they are beings from other dimensions. They came to help heal and rebuild our world. I have to go now."

I looked up and realized my sister had left. Then I noticed people I had not seen before walking around. It was like looking at a group of five people expanding to ten people in the blink of an eye.

Some of them carried clipboards. They would approach certain people, ask a few questions, and then guide them toward a group that seemed to be waiting for something.

Everything happened quickly after my dad's phone call; I was trying to figure out what was happening. Beings from other dimensions were here. The bigger question—did they come here to help or to harm?

The next moment, a person with a clipboard walked toward me. My body tensed up. Why were they singling out certain people?

As they approached me, the person asked, "You have multiple sclerosis. Is that correct?"

"How did you know? Why would that matter to you?"

They continued, "We did some research before we arrived. We are gathering people who may need more help."

Unsure about their motives, and still wary and a bit fearful of them, I made a request.

"I need to make a phone call first."

"Why? Who do you need to call?"

"I need to call a close friend to tell them that the Pink Ones are here."

They answered, "Your friend already knows. We are from the angelic realm. As soon as our parachutes hit the ground, we transformed into human bodies. This is happening right now, all over the world. We are here to help heal and rebuild."

Still uneasy, I walked with them to the group they had already assembled. I found out we were waiting for a minibus to transport us somewhere.

When the minibus arrived, we all got on.

I could hear the Pink Ones talking to each other. I looked around and realized no one was talking out loud.

Without thinking, I blurted out to them, "How can I understand what you are saying if you are not speaking out loud? Am I hearing you speak telepathically?"

"Yes, that is correct."

"And you are not censoring what you are saying in front of me?"

"No. We do not need to filter or hide our conversations. We are here to help."

I asked, "So, everyone on this bus has some type of health problem?"

"Yes. We want to take special care of those who may need extra help."

In the next part of the dream, my sister and I are getting settled in a motel room. Noticing several spirit animal figurines sitting on the top of a chest in the corner, I realized the spirit animals were there to protect and bring us messages.

First was a black jaguar, representing power, speed, and agility. When I looked up the symbolic significance of the jaguar, it made total sense it was in the dream. Jaguars help us understand the roads and patterns in our lives, especially during chaos. They also help us move to other dimensions and realms. Jaguars facilitate soul work, empowerment, psychic sight, and shape-shifting.

The next figurine was an otter. Known for enhancing creativity, transformation, and psychic abilities, the otter helps you navigate your emotional life with ease and joy. It also represents feminine power, grace, and good fortune.

The last one was a ferret, which assists us in reevaluating our life choices. They are keen observers with strong intuition. Their ability to see in the dark reminds you to use all your senses and offers inspiration and hope when struggling with dark times.

Since my father's message mentioned the "Pink Ones" and the angelic beings were using pink parachutes to arrive, I wanted to learn more about the spiritual significance of the color pink. Full of love, compassion, and feminine energy, the color pink is the high heart chakra. It makes us feel calm, nurtured, and accepted. Pink brings more positivity and hope into your life.

If I become discouraged or overwhelmed about the future of our world, I think about this dream. It is comforting to know help from other dimensions is coming.

This doesn't mean all we need to do is wait to be rescued. Focus on your personal growth and what you can do to help make our world a better place. Remember, the spirit world is waiting until more people awaken before they come. It is time we send a coherent message by our actions that we want help and are ready to receive it.

It is an exciting time to be on Earth. As you awaken, you will see and experience an amazing new way of living, filled with Divine guidance, light, and love. You will feel deeply connected. Claim your new life now—good health, abundance, happiness, passion, peace, prosperity, purpose, and joy.

Epilogue:
Whale Energy

———— ✦ ————

What an interesting journey this has been. I realized that whale energy describes my experience perfectly. Many believe the whale is the Record Keeper in the spirit world. Whale medicine people have a special DNA coding that allows sound frequencies to reveal ancient memories.

This makes so much sense to me! Music and sounds have always been important to me. When I got on the fast track of spiritual awakening after moving to Asheville, they began playing an even bigger role in my life. Listening to sacred music brought on an amazing kundalini awakening and spontaneous pineal activation. One of my favorite types of healing is sound healing. I always use music during my healing work.

Sound is a significant part of my prophetic visions. Often, a vision begins by hearing something a person says. Instinctively, I ask them to repeat what they said several times, and then a vision appears to me, like watching a movie. Later I realized it was not what they were saying, but the tone in their voice that triggered something in me to see the visions.

Most whale medicine people can hear frequencies not normally noticed. They have strong psychic skills, including the ability to communicate telepathically.

What caught my attention when learning about whale energy in the spirit world is that many whale peeps do not awaken their spiritual gifts unless it is time to access and use the memories. They also don't understand how they can do or know things like how to tap into the universal mind of Spirit. Gradually, it all becomes clear.

This explains a lot to me. Everything that happened was unexpected. When I started remembering ancient wisdom and how to use my spiritual abilities, I did not understand why or how this was happening. All I knew was to trust Spirit and remain open to whatever might show up.

As you continue your awakening and healing journey, here are a few simple spiritual truths to remember.

💜 **Listen to Your Guidance** 💜 **Remain Open** 💜

💜 **Trust Your Intuition** 💜

💜 **Trust the Universe** 💜

💜 **Surrender to Divine Timing** 💜

💜 **Do the Work** 💜 **Expect Miracles** 💜

Index

Acknowledgments

I am full of gratitude and appreciation for family, friends and colleagues who held the space of encouragement and support during the journey of writing this book. I could not have done it without you.

A special thanks to Anna Claudia Wachter, a millennial friend who convinced me to write this spiritual memoir.

Much gratitude to Caleb Beissert for contributing his poem *"A Light Shines"* and to Wendy Andrew, for the beautiful front cover art.

Especially thankful for all the professionals who helped me with their feedback and suggestions—beta readers, development editors, line editors, proofreaders, copy editor, cover designer, layout designer, Spanish translator and marketing consultants. I am eternally grateful to everyone who helped me turn an idea into a polished and engaging book.

About The Author

—⌇⌇⌇—

Chloe's extraordinary journey is filled with visions, lucid and prophetic dreams, parallel universes, collective dreaming and knowledge of past lives. She healed from deeply embedded trauma, an incurable illness, and serious medical conditions. Chloe shares major spiritual experiences she has had in Athens, Greece; Crete; Paris, France; Mexico; Ecuador; Egypt; and Asheville, NC. Chloe has performed intuitive energetic shamanic healing and mediumship sessions in the U.S., Mexico and Ecuador.

Chloe is an award-winning writer, creative director, multimedia artist, and former editor-in-chief and publisher of an award-winning magazine. She is now a Wisdom Keeper who can foresee and interpret Divine truth. Her connections with Spirit Guides in other dimensions bring cosmic knowledge to her ancient wisdom.

Chloe's psychic abilities include:

- **clairvoyance** – sees beyond ordinary perception
- **clairaudience** – hears messages from the spirit world
- **prophecy** – perceives future events
- **remote viewing** – connects and heals from a distance
- **telepathy** – sends and receives thoughts via extrasensory energy
- **clairsentience** – uses strong intuition that gives information and warnings from the spirit world.

"The intense healing I received from Chloe helped to open me up to past life traumas and grief and to clear karma so that my current life can progress without continuing to carry burdens from the past. I feel lighter and free to better continue this life's journey as a Lightworker. I felt surrounded by a healing golden light. In the days and nights after, I experienced vivid dreams and visions that helped to process past grief and prepare me for the work that is to come. I highly recommend this healing experience for anyone — especially all Lightworkers, Star Seeds and Indigos." **—C. P., Registered Nurse**

"Thank you, Chloe, for the healing session. I definitely felt a shift during and after our session and there's no doubt it had something to do with the positive results I received at my doctor's appointment. You are a true healer. Every little touch — from the music, crystals, rattle, feather, and even the cards for affirmations afterwards — created such a safe and sacred place for me. You are a beacon of light and love. I always feel blessed to be in your presence; you continually remind me of the Divine." **— K. M.**

www.ChloeKempWisdomKeeper.com

www.ingramcontent.com/pod-product-compliance
Lightning Source LLC
Chambersburg PA
CBHW020444130626
46549CB00001B/293